PRIVATE EYE ANNUAL 2012

EDITED BY IAN HISLOP

"Tsk. The modern media is obsessed with sex and violence"

Published in Great Britain by
Private Eye Productions Ltd
6 Carlisle Street, London W1D 3BN
www.private-eye.co.uk

© 2012 Pressdram Ltd
ISBN 978-1-901784-57-2
Designed by Bridget Tisdall
Printed and bound in Great Britain by
Butler Tanner & Dennis, Frome, Somerset
2 4 6 8 10 9 7 5 3 1

MIX
Paper from
responsible sources
FSC® C023561

PRIVATE EYE ANNUAL 2012

EDITED BY IAN HISLOP

"Honestly, it's enough to make you smile"

NEW FROM GNOME – YOUR NEXT BOX SET!

Over 4,000 hours of the Leveson Inquiry in a 94 disc collection!

Relive every single amazing moment of this groundbreaking inquiry which has become the must-see television event of the decade.

And enjoy once again the series' great catchphrase *"Please turn to bullet point 3, under briefing paper 7, paragraph 36, page 7,503... have you got it yet? It's under tab 9 in the previous file, on page 10,976...!"*

● *INCLUDES* Cast interviews, audio commentary by Lord Leveson and deleted scenes featuring Piers Moron.

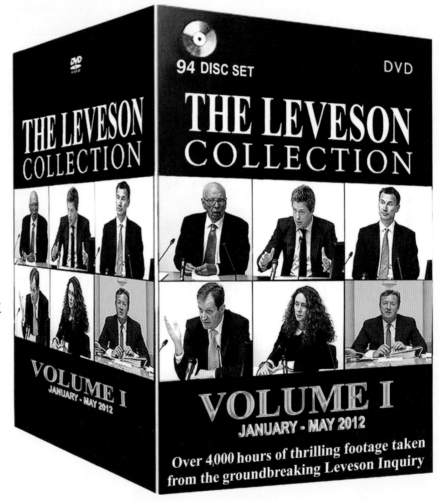

Price: £994.99

WILL THE RECESSION TRIGGER A RECESSION?

THE Chancellor George Osborne last night brushed aside warnings from the Governor of the Bank of England that the current recession could trigger a recession in the British economy.

"When I look around me and I see a country caught in the grip of a recession, I see no reason to suggest that this country is about to fall into recession.

"The doom-mongers may see things differently, but I believe that we'll steer clear of a recession and instead enjoy a sustained period of steadily deepening recession."

GREECE WILL MISS TARGET

THE Greek government admitted today that it would miss its target demanded by the troika of lenders to utterly obliterate its economy and create 100% unemployment.

"While we have made major steps towards the total destruction of our country, much work remains to be done," admitted a scared-looking Government spokesman having petrol bombs hurled at him. "I've just sacked myself, does that help?"

The troika said the total collapse of the Greek economy must be achieved if Greece is to qualify for billions more euros in loans which are needed to keep the country going due to the total collapse of the Greek economy.

BANK OF ENGLAND ANNOUNCES MORE QI

THE Monetary Policy Committee says it will pump seventy-five billion new episodes of QI onto our screens in an attempt to kick-start the economy.

"We're confident that while £200bn of QE failed to stop the country sliding into an abyss," said a wee Scottish man, "the injection of Stephen Fry will be just the shot in the arm our ailing economy needs.

"When you look at the mess we're in, you can hardly blame us for coming to the conclusion that only QI can save us now."

GOVE-GATE LATEST

By Our Political Staff **E. Mail**

WHITEHALL was seething last night after it had been revealed that Education Secretary Michael Gove had been sending "private emails" which had not been shown to his civil servants.

"This is absolutely outrageous and probably illegal," said one top Whitehall insider. "If we do not see these messages, we cannot stop the minister doing what he wants to do."

The Gove-gate scandal came to light when it emerged that the education secretary had last February sent emails to his special advisers, Henry de Pinstripe-Zoot (who is married to Daily Telegraph columnist, Lady Rowan Atkinson-Pelling) and Melina Narozanski-Huffington-Strassinopoulos-Theodorakopoulos-Smith. Some of the emails concerned the potentially explosive issue of plans to set up a free school by the former Daily Telegraph commentator, Simon Heffer, which included compulsory cricket for a minimum 18 hours a week and readings at Assembly from the works of Enoch Powell.

Additionally, Gove had sent g-mails to his staffers on this same sensitive issue, using the name "Mrs Cherie Blurt", in order to hide his identity from Whitehall mandarins who were monitoring his Blackberry hotmail account in order to *(cont. p. 94)*

EUROZONE CRISIS

So, we're all agreed. We don't know what to do

"Mum, can you run me next door?"

School news

St Cake's Free School

Gove Term begins today. There are 250 middle class pupils in the school. R.J. Pushy-Parent is Head of Portakabins. D.T. Sharpe-Elbows is keeper of the Portaloos. Mr G.B.Y. Chips has been brought out of retirement to become Headmaster and to teach compulsory Latin to the Romulans (Year 7) and the Remans (Year 8). Ms Suzuki-Method is in charge of Hot House.

Parents' evening will be every evening. Parents who fail to complete homework will be given detention supervised by Brigadier S.A.S. Balaclava (retired) who is in charge of school discipline.

Spectators will be read in the school library (formerly the Bus Shelter) on Thursdays.

Founder's day will be held on The Feast of St Toby, November 22.

The School Run will commence at 7.30am, 4x4s will be parked outside the school gates (double yellow lines only please).

HAS TORY SWEETHEART HAD A FACELIFT? YOU DECIDE

Before

After

Clarke Announces 'Biggest Revolution In Court Reporting History'

What you will see when TV cameras are at last allowed into Britain's courtrooms

(Close-up of old man in wig)

Mr Justice Cocklecarrot

(for it is he): Good evening, ladies and gentlemen, and welcome to Strictly Come Judging! As you know, under Mr Clarke's new rules you're only allowed to see me giving my judgement and not all the boring stuff that's gone beforehand. *(He points to pile of "bundles")*. So, let's get on with the judging! The case that I've been listening to for the last 14 days concerns the deeply shocking affair of the theft of a paperclip, carrying the monetary value of 1p, from Mr Patel's newsagency on Pricerite Road, Neasden, by Mr Dwayne Hoodie of no fixed abode. Rarely has this court heard a more disturbing and depressing catalogue of depravity as has been evidenced by this sorry tale, which viewers have rightly not been permitted by Mr Clarke to see, as it would undoubtedly have caused distress across the entire nation. Suffice it to say that, having listened carefully to the evidence (although I may on occasion have inadvertently given the impression that I was asleep), and having weighed up very carefully the competing arguments of learned Counsel, including the disastrously incompetent defence offered by Mr Winston Probono, and the excellent and superbly argued case put for the prosecution by that very promising newcomer to the bar, my nephew Mr Simeon Cocklecarrot-Starborgling, I have had no hesitation in reaching my verdict.

(Caption appears on screen: "Some viewers may find the following scenes distressing")

(Judge puts on black cap)

Dwayne Hoodie, you have committed an abominable crime for which it is only right that you should face the full rigour of the law. I hereby sentence you to be taken from this place, issued with a broom and made to serve no less than two hours of community service in what remains of Pricerite Road. And may God have mercy on your soul.

England Rioters 'Poor And Young'

COMPREHENSIVE statistics on the England riots show those charged with offences were poorer, younger and of lower educational achievement than average.

ON OTHER PAGES

● Pope 'More Catholic than other people who aren't Catholic'
● Bear 'Still shitting in woods'

"Yes, our council is very slow with adoptions"

BIRCH

THE EYE'S MOST READ STORIES

Afghanistan War Celebrates 10th Anniversary

THERE were joyous scenes across Afghanistan with Taliban forces detonating hundreds of car bombs as the long-running war celebrates its 10th anniversary.

"It seems so funny to think that when the war started President Bush thought it would only last six months at best," said one Taliban leader, "but we were always confident this war would run and run."

President Obama added his congratulations to the war, "When the conflict started, Afghanistan was a lawless, war-torn land bereft of hope with a population living in fear, but now we have transformed it into a lawless, war-torn land bereft of hope with a population living in absolute fear.

"Congratulations to everyone involved in Operation Endless Quagmire."

President Karzai also sent a message to all Afghans which read simply "Please Don't Kill Me".

Army to Discipline Baha Mousa Soldiers

The Army has insisted the nineteen soldiers identified to have taken part in the torture and killing of the Iraqi hotel receptionist Baha Mousa in Basra in 2003 will now be severely punished.

"We've already woken them in the dead of night in their barracks and dragged them from their beds with hoods placed over their heads," said a senior General. "They'll now be kept in the ski position with legs apart and bent at 45 degrees with hands raised whilst being kicked in the genitals and kidneys for the next 48 hours.

"We believe firm action like this is the only way to send out a clear message to the rest of our servicemen that abhorrent acts of torture will never be tolerated by the British Army."

GLENDA SLAGG
Fleet Street's Top Fe-mail On Sunday!

■ Spare a thought for blushin' bride Zara – Princess Anne's Daughter stoopid!!? It seems like only yesterday she was tying the knot with England's top rugger bugger Mike Tindall?!! And now before the bubbly's gone flat her hunk of a hubby is caught havin' a ruck with a hooker in a seedy nightclub (Geddit?!?!!) What a disgrace?!?! Take a tip from Auntie Glenda darling?!! Boot him into touch – that'll be his penalty for trying to score away from home?!!!? Geddit??!!?

■ Grow up Zara!!! OK, so scrummy hubby Mike went a-boozin' and a-floozin' along with his rugby pals!?!

What does she expect ??!! Who did she think she was marrying?!? A.N. Wilson???! Get off yer high horse darling (Geddit??!)and let boys be boys!!? All together now, "Four and twenty virgins came down from Mike Tindall's Hotel Room"!!!

■ Come off it Dame Helen?!!!? Who do you think you're trying to kid with your poor-little-me snapped-in-my-bikini number??!!? You're only whingin' about it so we all print the photo again so everyone can see how good you look!!?! Methinks the Dame doth protest too much!!? That's Shakespeare stoopid!!!

Byeee!!

7

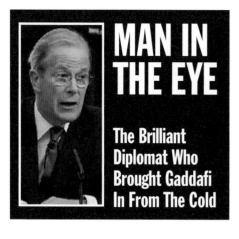

MAN IN THE EYE

The Brilliant Diplomat Who Brought Gaddafi In From The Cold

HE MAY not be a household name, but **Sir Mark Spookington-Allen** is the man who brought off perhaps the most amazing diplomatic coup of modern times.

It was he who in 2004, as head of MI6's Libya desk, persuaded Colonel Gaddafi to renounce his programme to develop weapons of mass destruction in return for "whatever he wanted".

A brilliant Oxford scholar, Sir Mark spoke 17 languages, ranging from Inuit to Ancient Norse.

A lifelong Arabist, he once trekked across the notorious sand dunes of the Nogud Desert on a camel, accompanied only by a Tuareg retainer whom he playfully named "Geoffrey" after his cricketing hero Geoffrey Boycott.

Colleagues describe Sir Mark as "incredibly clever", "intensely charming" and "able to do the Times crossword in less than two minutes".

The letter from Sir Mark discovered in the ruins of the British Embassy in Tripoli, in a box marked "Highly Confidential – MI6 stuff", shows the astonishing diplomatic skills which have long marked him out as one of the ablest players of the realpolitik game of his generation.

This is the full text of the letter that was to change history:

My dear Muammar (if I may),

Just a line to let you know how much Tony and I look forward to meeting you to finalise the deal which will bring our two great countries closer together than ever before.

I suggest that we stage "the historic handshake" in one of your wonderful Bedouin tents. We English love a good tent, you know, it must be all those marquees at village fêtes and camping holidays with the Scouts on Dartmoor, and it'll go down a storm with the so-called "gentlemen of the press"! Particularly if you throw in some of your uniformed lovelies!

Just to remind you what the deal is that we mapped out on the back of that envelope last month:

1. We drop all the sanctioning nonsense and release all that $217 million held by NatWest.

2. We hand over the Lockerbie chap, on the grounds that he's suffering from an incurable cold or something.

3. We round up all those Libyan troublemakers living in Britain whom your people so kindly listed for us, and send them back to you – on condition, of course, that they won't be tortured or anything disagreeable like that.

In return for all this:

1. You very generously agree to give up all those "weapons of mass destruction" (which, of course, you don't have, but Tony is very keen on this after his recent spot of bother in Iraq).

2. You promise not to murder any more British policewomen or to send any more guns to the IRA. You and I know, of course, that this is all ancient history. But it'll look good at our end.

3. (The important bit!) You give all the oil and gas concessions we were talking about to our friends at BP (usual cut for yourself and charming family!).

I think that covers everything. Can't wait to tuck into a plate of sheep's eyes at the feast. Tony has asked me to send you his warmest greetings, and hopes you will enjoy the complete DVD set of Sex and the City, of which he knows you are a big fan!

Sorry this letter is in English, but none of our chaps speak Arabic, and even mine is a bit rusty, if truth be told!

Inshallah!

Spookington-Allen of Arabia

PS. I've had a word with my friends at the LSE and they tell me they'd be delighted to give a First Class Honours Degree and a PhD in Heart Surgery and Rocket Science to your delightful son, Shufti. The Vice-Chancellor, incidentally, thanks you for your very generous cheque!

● Sir Mark Spookington-Allen has now left the Foreign Office, and is working as an international consultant for BP.

"Ah, Mr Bond – you phoned about a kitten"

HUNTER

CLARKSON SAT NAV TEETHING PROBLEMS

Turn right... then turn right again... keep going right until you're just to the right of Genghis Khan... keep going right...

DIARY

ED BALLS: MY SOFTER SIDE

Kids? I love 'em. Reciting my very favourite nursery rhymes to them at bedtime is one of the very real joys of my life.

"Jack and Jill went up the hill
To fetch a pail of water
Jack fell down and smashed his crown and there was blood all over the place and serve him right because he was a little wanker and deserved all he bloody got.
And Jill came tumbling after."

They look back at me with their bright, trusting little eyes, and sometimes – you know what? – I find myself welling up.

When I'm finished, I encourage the kids to have a full and open discussion on the long-term implications of these rhymes.

It is my belief that no child should be held back in life because of a lack of engagement by adults.

I'm sorry, but if a kid wants to say something, them I'm not going to stand in its way.

So I give them a fair hearing but to be honest they don't have the foggiest, not the fucking foggiest, and it's my duty as a highly intelligent adult to interrupt them when they get it wrong.

Like, the other night, one of them said she felt sorry for poor Jack falling down that hill, and I said, gently and lovingly, "Oi, less of the poor Jack, sorry's got nothing to do with it, he was crap – no, let me finish – the guy was complete and utter crap, total rubbish, and if he can't even carry a pail of water down a bloody hill then he shouldn't start whining and snivelling when he comes a cropper, no, let me finish, he screwed up on the whole bucket-filling process, face it, he doesn't know the first thing about buckets, so now he's got what he deserves. Get over it!"

It's what education's all about, and when I looked back at those innocent little eyes, I saw that that little fellow was welling up, just like me, so moved and so grateful was he for my lovely little lesson.

Bless!

The Sound of Music must be my absolute favouritest film of all time. I'm sorry, guys, but just thinking about it makes me well up. My Favourite Things is the song I've always strived to live my life by. It's just got everything I cherish most, everything I care about in this great big wonderful world of ours –

"Girls in white dresses with blue satin sashes
Snowflakes that stay on my nose and eyelashes
Silver white winters that melt into springs
These are a few of my favourite things
When the dog bites
When the bee stings
I have the dog put down
And I stamp on the bee till it's well and truly crushed
And then I don't feel so bad."

Have you ever baked a Victoria sponge? It's one of my favourite pastimes, and a really super way to unwind after a hard day's rough-and-tumble on the floor of the House of Commons.

Ingredients: 8oz of butter or margarine, softened at room temperature.
8oz of caster sugar
4 medium eggs
2tsp vanilla extract
8oz self-raising flour
milk

1. Mix the butter and the sugar together in a bowl. I always find the best way to do this is to punch them with both fists, over and over again, really give them a good going over, teach them a lesson they'll never forget, not for a long while.

2. Beat in the eggs until they're screaming at you, begging you to stop. As I say, I always believe in working very closely with the eggs.

3. Fold in the flour using a large metal spoon, a sharp knife, a hammer and a pair of pliers.

4. Bake for 20-25 minutes. Serve with jam and whipped cream. If anyone says they don't like it for any reason, then it's always been my firm belief that this is their absolute and inalienable right so be sure to give them a fair hearing before telling them to fuck the fuck off.

I have a sweet and innocent, I'd almost say childlike side to my character, which the media ignores at its peril. It's not widely known, for instance, that I welcome any chance to play Cat's Cradle, which is a really super game to play, particularly with the very young. You just thread some wool between their fingers and across their hands – you should see their little faces! – and then when they're completely tied up you can get on with more important things and they can't do a fucking thing about it. Bless!

As told to CRAIG BROWN

The Secret DIARY OF SIR JOHN MAJOR

I was not inconsiderably annoyed when my wife Norman remarked over breakfast when I was enjoying a bowl of my favourite Red Berries Special K cereal, "I expect you will be staying in tonight to watch television, John."

I said that there was no particular reason why I would be making such a decision, in my judgement. "The cricket season is over, Norman, and the England team have acquitted themselves in no small measure favourably."

"No," she said as she poured a jug of coffee over my Red Berries cereal, "It is not the cricket highlights to which I refer but the return of the popular reality entertainment show Strictly Come Dancing."

"Why would I be wishing to watch that?" I enquired innocently through a mouthful of somewhat soggy berries.

"Do not play the innocent with me," she said. "That frightful woman is on, dressed up in sequins and making a fool of herself."

"Not Ann Widdecombe?" I replied in a jocular manner.

"Oh no! You didn't have an affair with her as well, did you?" Norman riposted, pouring yet more coffee onto the Red Berries which were now not inconsiderably brown. Oh yes.

"It takes two to tango," she observed as she left the room slamming the door behind her, "or in your case, three."

EDWINA CURRIE'S STRICTLY SHOCKER

...and what did John Major do next?

PUNCH AND JOURNEY

K.J.Lamb

"It's been emotional… I've come so far… when I think back… sob…"

GYPSY STORY REFUSES TO LEAVE FRONT PAGE

by Our Travelling Staff
Dale Farm

THE story about travellers which set up on the front page of this newspaper two weeks ago is still stubbornly refusing to move on.

Said a frustrated editor, "We want to put the story on an alternative site, such as page 94, which seems to me perfectly reasonable."

But the story will not be budged and is remaining fixed, ruining the view of the more attractive pieces about Sienna Miller at London Fashion Week.

Said a spokesman for the story, "It is our basic human right to invade the front page and to stay there for as long as we like.

"It is part of the tradition and culture of travelling people that their stories should suddenly appear and refuse to travel anywhere."

Stories about anarchists are now joining the stories about travellers and there are worries that quite soon there will be no room even for stories about Downton Abbey and (cont. p. 94)

THE ALTERNATIVE VOICE

DAVE SPART Co-Chair of the Tufnell Park Friends of the Romany and No To The Badger Cull Coalition.

Once again it is totally sickening to see the forces of reaction showing their true neo-Nazi colours with their brutal eviction of thousands of totally innocent members of the travelling community who have perfectly legitimately occupied a field in Essex as is their basic human right under the European Convention on the Right To Romany to which Britain is a signatory... er... not since the ethnic cleansing of thousands of innocent Serbs in Blair's Bosnian war has there been such a savage and flagrant attack on basic human dignity, which is totally exactly the same as Hitler's notorious pogroms against minority groups including gypsies, gays and Communists... er... Basildon Council should be tried at the International Criminal Court for war crimes and genocide which the UN has ruled this totally is which means (cont. p. 94)

RESPECT OUR CULTURE

WE ♥ DALE FARM

WE'RE TRAVELLERS AND WE'RE NOT GOING ANYWHERE!

Ariss

Daily Mail

AN APOLOGY

In recent weeks, months and years we may have given the mistaken impression that Gypsies weren't the nicest of people through headlines such as 'THIEVING GYPO SCUM MAKE LIFE FOR DECENT PEOPLE HELL' and 'GYPO NIGHTMARE MADE WORSE BY ARRIVAL OF NIGHTMARISH GYPOS WHO WILL PROBABLY KILL YOU IN YOUR SLEEP'.

We now realise, in the light of there being two fruity young gypsies in crop tops at Dale Farm whom we could put on the front page, nothing could be further from the truth, as gypsies are in fact a proud people with a long tradition of wearing very little clothes and being fruity.

We apologise for any confusion and any confusion in the future when we demand to know where the fruity young gypo stole that watch from.

 **la Repubica**

30 SEPTEMBER 2011   4 million euros

Britain shamed by Borisconi's antics

by Our Man In London **Jim Naughtie-Naughtie**

A sensational new book has become the talking point of London by revealing that the city's controversial Mayor, Silvio Borisconi, has been guilty of a string of serial infidelities and inappropriate advances to young women.

The tousle-haired Borisconi last night attempted to downplay the book's lurid allegations about his private life by describing them as a "pile of piff paff" and "absolute Tommy rot".

After years of tolerating the Mayor's sexual indiscretions, there are now clear signs that the public is getting seriously impatient with his carryings-on.

Routemistresses

Said one ordinary Londoner, Ken Livingstone, 76, "He is making Britain a laughing stock. No one believes that Borisconi can tackle London's problems, when he is too busy cavorting with inappropriate younger women and having love children – he should leave that kind of thing to me."

But Mayor Borisconi is unrepentant. "Everyone knows what I'm like," he said, "I'm a red-blooded Englishman. What do you expect? People love me and soon they will get rid of that effete, politically-correct weed Cameron and choose a real three-times-a-night kind of man to be their leader."

● See pics of Borisconi's "Bunga-Bunga Babes" p. 94

Markets Remain Calm As Italy wins Triple X Rating

By Our Economics Staff **Robert Pesto**

ITALY yesterday became the first member of the eurozone to be upgraded to a full XXX rating by the agency Low Standards and Phwoar.

Italy's shock new status follows revelations of a sharp increase in public money spent on official bunga-bunga parties, and soaring imports of young women from Britain.

Italy has now been declared an "unsafe haven" for any girl below the age of 50.

Silvio Berlusconi is 94.

SEX-CRAZED AMERICAN DRUG FIEND FREED TO MAKE MILLIONS

by Our Perugia Court Staff
A.A. Gillty and **James Murder**

FORMER murderer Foxy Knoxy last night walked free into the arms of waiting publishers and Hollywood agents, after a bunch of illiterate Italian peasants inexplicably found her innocent of committing one of the most gruesome murders in the history of crime.

But as Foxy Knoxy escapes the clutches of the Italian justice system, a series of disturbing questions remain unanswered.

Those disturbing unanswered questions in full

1. Why was she smiling when she heard the jury's "innocent" verdict?

2. Why when she left the court was she weeping tears of guilt?

3. Why did the prosecution fail to present any evidence which would have proved her guilt?

4. Was the judge bribed by Mafia agents working for US PR companies hired by millionaire supporters of the influential Knox family?

5. Why did Knox have a telltale hole in her jumper when she left the court?

6. If Knox wasn't the murderer, then who was – apart from the mysterious African drug dealer who was gaoled for the crime four years ago?

7. What really happened at the wild, drug-fuelled sex party that never took place?

8. Why does the Daily Mail go on printing this drivel every day?

What Foxy Knoxy will do next

It is already clear that, thanks to this blunder by the notoriously corrupt Italian justice system, Knox will soon be the 14th richest woman in America.

What she stands to gain

● A rumoured Tony Blair-style book deal with Rupert Murdoch's HarperCollins could net her $25 million.

● A blockbuster Hollywood movie of her story, directed by Roman "Paedo" Polanski and starring Meryl Streep could make her upwards of $100 million.

● Already being negotiated by Knox's agents are a series of mega-sponsorship deals for fashion and beauty products, including L'Oreal, Chanel and lingerie from Victoria's Secret.

● An exclusive two-hour primetime interview with CNN's star presenter Piers Moron could land her a fee of $2.50, which she might well present to charity.

● But Knoxy's biggest reward of all could be her $25 trillion compensation claim against the Italian government which could trigger an Italian sovereign debt default, leading to the collapse of the euro and the disintegration of the entire world economy.

The Mail Says

This entire charade is nothing more than an outrageous slap in the face for the real victim of the crime, British girl *(fill in name, please, subs)*

On other pages

■ Foreign man whose name doesn't rhyme with 'Foxy' also released **94**

PLUS ■ Why oh why is evil Lockerbie bomber al-Megrahi still alive? Come on and die, you bastard **2** ■ What happened to good, old-fashioned British politeness? asks Melanie Phillips **3**

ME AND MY SPOON
THIS WEEK

KATE WINSLET

Do you have a favourite spoon?

(Screams) Oh my God. I wasn't expecting this... I never thought I'd be asked to do Me and My Spoon.

So, do you have a favourite spoon?

I can't believe this is happening *(gasp)*. It's me doing Me and My Spoon. Thank you, thank you all so much for asking me *(pant)*. This means so much to me.

As I said, do you have a favourite spoon?

It's not about me and which spoon I like. It's my fabulous producers and fellow fabulous actors and fabulous HBO and fabulous everyone who have all been so fabulous *(sigh)*... they should be here talking about *their* spoons not me *(laughs)*.

To put it another way, spoonwise do you have a favourite?

I'd like to dedicate all my spoon answers to the person who made it all possible, my mum *(sob)*, because however old you are, you still need your mum's spoon, so mum *(gulp)*, this is for you. Thank you, thank you, thank you.

Has anything amusing ever happened to you in connection with a spoon?

Oh my God, you've asked me if anything amusing has ever happened to me in connection with a spoon... is this real? God *(screams)*...

Thank you, thank you, Kate. Thank you, I never thought I would ever interview you... oh my God... it's me and Kate Winslet. I'd like to thank my fabulous edtior, all my fabulous sub-editors, Ray on the picture desk, all the others, you know who you are, and all my readers and my mum, without whom *(You're fired. Ed.)*

NEXT WEEK: *Abi Titmuss, "Me and My Abbey".*

11

FOXY FOXY IS HE INNOCENT?
DEFENCE SECRETARY DEFENDS HIMSELF

"I'm not a boy wonder – I'm his special adviser"

Report by Sir Augustus O'Donnell, the Head of the Civil Service on the Conduct of the Secretary of State for Defence, the Rt Hon Dr Liam Fox

1. I have been asked by the Prime Minister to enquire into the conflict while in office of Dr Fox and his friend Mr Adam Werritty and in particular whether this relationship posed a grave threat to world peace and the vital interests of the United Kingdom.

2. After interviewing Dr Fox, I am assured that he acted in good faith and without any pecuniary motivation throughout this affair (not that it was an affair, I hasten to add, nor is it in my remit in any way to speculate about the exact nature of the relationship between Dr Fox and his much younger male friend).

3. I am further convinced that Dr Fox was guilty only of a serious failure of judgement in allowing his young flatmate to use the official Ministry of Defence trouser press on no less than 18 separate occasions, and to do so without being subjected to the correct vetting procedure and given full security clearance.

4. I am further minded to find that Dr Fox acted in breach of the ministerial code, particularly in respect of article 17 (b) which lays down clear guidelines with regard to use by unauthorised personnel of ministerial equipment, such as the aforesaid trouser press.

5. However, I am satisfied that despite Dr Fox's inappropriate behaviour in respect of the trouser press, he was not in any way guilty of certain other allegations which have been made against him, namely that he was acting for shady, neo-con, far-right political interests who were aiming to overthrow the government of Iran with the aid of the Sri Lankans and the Royal Family of Dubai, with whom Dr Fox and his young friend stayed on a number of occasions, although no impropriety occurred, nor would it be any of my business if it had done so, which it did not.

6. All of which leads me to conclude, as I have been asked to by the prime minister, that it would be right for Dr Fox to resign before he caused the prime minister any further embarrassment.

7. This matter is now closed and the purpose of my report is to draw a line under it, allowing the nation and the government to move on.

Signed

G.O.D.

Appendix One

It has not been within the remit of this inquiry to look into questions relating to the influence exercised on government by lobbyists acting for powerful commercial interests – in particular the role of Pargav, Negev, Satnav, Mossad etc. All these matters are to be fully investigated by the public inquiry into the culture of lobbying which is being conducted by Mr Justice Long-Grass and is expected to report not later than 2094.

Old Possum's Book of Fat Cats

(with grateful acknowledgement to TS Eliot)

That Werritty's a mystery bloke – his card says he's a SPAD.
Turns out he's nothing of the sort, it looks like we've been had.
But he's a friend of Liam Fox – perhaps that should say 'was'.
They sometimes met three times a week – no reason: just because.

Werritty, oh Werritty, there's no one quite like Werritty.
Denies he's broken any laws, although he looks quite ferretty.
But when the lobbyists are out or a freebie's in the air
Look closely at the photos: Adam Werritty was there.

He had meetings at the MoD, flew halfway round the world.
If I tell you what they talked about you'll find your toes have curled.
You won't spot him in the hallway, you won't meet him on the stair
But when you check the footage: Adam Werritty was there.

He had access to the diary – he could tell you where and when
You could meet with Liam Fox and other quite important men.
A four-star US general has some thoughts he'd like to share?
In a restaurant? In Florida? Get Werritty out there!

Werritty, oh Werritty – what will he do now, Werritty?
A man who overlooked such unimportant things as verity.
Will businessmen still call him? And will anybody care
If we find, when this is over… Adam Werritty's not there.

The NOGBAD Connection

Who is he, the shadowy figure behind the Cayman Islands-registered company NOGBAD, the board of which includes such world-famous names as Conrad Black, Henry Kissinger and Sarah Palin? The Chairman of NOGBAD is the Israeli real-estate tycoon, Badman Nogudovich. But even he may only be a front for the real power behind the NOGBAD organisation, the mysterious charitable foundation, the Atlantic Bridge Club, set up in 2009 to promote the playing of bridge between Senior North Atlantic political figures, or possibly to facilitate the construction of an enormous, 300-mile-long bridge linking London and Washington. Or possibly just to put money into the Abu Dhabi registered bank account of Dr Fox's personal security adviser Mr Adam Werritty, who in March 2010 checked into the 5-Star Shufti Al Krukhi hotel in (cont. p. 94)

(cont. p. 94)

FOX BLAMES MEDIA

Bitter? Of course not

John Specht, being VICE President of the Spearmint Rhino, did no more than invite the lady scholars to immodestly disport themselves to fund their studies. Inasmuch and insofar as they did so do, then they did no more than incite adultery, for the lust of a hapless man who lusteth after woman hath committed adultery in his heart. (Matthew5:28) Such harlotry did no more than Bring Mammon To His Knees In The City of London, for by means of a harlot a man is reduced to a crust of bread (Proverbs 6:26) – *Mr_Salmon*

spot on samon the bank's spend ARE MONEY entertaining client's in lap dancing club's TALK ABOUT PR GAFF'S but think of the good will if they invite US THE MUG PUNTER'S maybe one dance per person plus extra's for long standing customer's? – *gash_hunter*

As a student myself (self-taught), I was delighted to hear that a Lapp dancing club was opening in my neighbourhood. Braving the angry insults of the philistines assembled outside, I entered the establishment with my friend Edwin. Suffice to say I struggled to detect the sound of a single kantele, jouhikko or säkipilli amid the cacophony that assailed my ears. As for dancing, there was nary a polka to be seen, although three burly members of staff performed an impromptu "bull dance" with my friend Edwin. His costume, which replicated the spiny contours of the fertility god Varalden Omai, was alleged to have "upset the girls", whose scanty regalia I confess I have yet to fathom. I have since returned a dozen or so times, but regret to report that it has not improved. – *Cecil*

I am not a student, but I WOULD BE A LAP DANCER IF THE CUSTOMER WAS TIM HENMAN! ☺ Tim is a gentleman and he would never put his mucky paws all over you, not that Tim has mucky paws of course, he's so nice and clean! Not that Tim goes to lap dancing clubs anyway, I don't think it would go down well with The Lovely Lucy (grrr!)●. I know she's blonde but I always picture Tim with a big huggable brunette (like me!) ● – *Tor*

Why do they go to these sordid places? It's so serious, with none of the camaraderie and banter you get from dogging. My wife and I have many hobbies, including real ale and non-league football, but dogging is best. Give us a wet Wednesday in Cannock Chase any day! – *Dogger_Bank*

This afternoon I bought a pint of milk, an evening paper and a lap dance from a Lithuanian medical student, all for £21. How many Russians can say that? – *Born_free*

Apple Man Dead

BY STEVE 'BOOK OF' JOBS

THE world was in mourning last night for the most important man in the entire history of humanity.

Tributes poured in for the figure described as "the single most influential thinker ever." Typical of the praise was one appleman fan, Eve, who said:

"Adam was a creative genius. He came up with the names for everything, animals, birds, plants, flowers… the lot."

She continued, "He opened the door to a world of knowledge… or a tree anyway."

Adam will of course always be best remembered for the apple which some critics have claimed may not have been "an unqualified force for good." One, a Mr Snake, said that, "Yes, the apple changed everything about the way we live but not necessarily for the better in *(cont. 94,000 BC.)*

"Sometimes I think going to university and getting a degree was just a waste of time and money"

That Honorary Degree Citation In Full

SALUTAMUS KYLIEAM MINOGUEAM CANTORAM ANTIPODIENSEM ET 'REGINA POPPA' AUTEM THESPIANA CELEBRISSIMA PER OPERA SAPONICA AUSTRALIENSIS 'VICINI' ET CANTATIT MULTI CARMINAE FAMOSAE PER EXEMPLA 'EGO SIM FORTUNATA – FORTUNATA FORTUNATA FORTUNATA', ET 'NON POSSUM TE EXPELLERE MEA CAPUT' ET 'ROTATI CIRCUM'. MINOGUEA MAJORA SYMBOLA SEXUA EST ET ICONA HOMOSEXUALORUM STATUA APUD 'DOMINA TUSSAUDA' POPULARI EST PER GLUTEA MINIMA PERTISSIMA PER DELECTATI PATRONARUM. SORORE DANNII MINOGUEA JUDICATRICE 'X FACTOR' ET NUM KYLIEA ALUMNA ANGLIA RUSKIN EST ET GAUDEAMUS IGITUR!

HALO!

● Friday 16 SEPTEMBER 2011

MYSTERY FIGURE AT JORDAN BAPTISM REVEALED

by Our Religious Staff ST MATTHEW PARRIS

Who was the mysterious "man in white" who, witnesses claim, walked amongst them at the baptism ceremony for Rupert Murdoch's daughters, Grace and Favour, held on the banks of the river Jordan last year?

Although many pictures have been published of the historic ceremony, showing a host of celebrities gathered by the waters of the world's most holiest river – including Nicole Kidman and the Queen of Jordan – not one of them showed the "man in white apparel" who witnesses swear appeared at the ceremony to offer his blessing.

But now, the children's mother, Ms Wendi Deng, 26, has confessed to the fashion bible Vogue that the "angelic figure in white" who graciously agreed to act as the "Son-of-Godfather" to her daughters was not Jesus, as so many had supposed, but the Rev Tony Blair, formerly vicar of St Albion's, and now the Chairman of the global multi-faith religious body DAFT (Drawing All Faiths Together).

According to witnesses, following the baptism "the heavens opened and a mighty shower of money descended onto the vicar's head", while an Australian voice boomed out, "This is my beloved mate, Tony, in whom I am well pleased".

The Rev Blair then apparently attempted to walk on the river's waters, but fell in and had to be rescued from drowning by the prompt intervention of the Royal Jordanian Lifeboat Institution.

When asked why no photographic record of his appearance at the gathering had ever appeared before, the Rev Blair's office explained, "It's a miracle. It's like the Turin Shroud in reverse. In fact, Tony is everywhere at all times. But we can't see him because he's too busy making money."

"'Fucking tosser' is an oxymoron. Have we not taught you ANYTHING?!"

IN THE COURTS

Oligarkhovich v. Beririchovsky. Before Mr Justice Cocklecarrot. Day 1.

Sir Jonathan Hugefee: My Lord, I represent Mr Roman Oligarkhovich, one of the richest clients it has ever been my privilege to represent.

Mr Justice Cocklecarrot: And which of these two Russian gentlemen is he? Is he the one who owns a football club? Or is he the other one?

Hugefee: My Lord, it is true that my client is the proud owner of the Chelsea Football Club. But I must point out that this is not strictly relevant to the case before you – unless, of course, my learned friend attempts to drag it in, in an effort to discredit my client by suggesting that he is no more than an obscenely rich playboy and dilettante, who swans about on luxury yachts with women half his age and behaves like an overpaid premiership footballer.

Mr Lawrence Cashinowicz *(for Mr Beririchovsky)*: That is indeed the gravamen of our case, My Lord. But we shall further show that in his capacity as co-owner of the prestigious Siberian-based oil company, Sibtheft, Mr Oligarkhovich successfully blackmailed my client by threatening that, unless my client handed over his share of the business, he would get his friend President Putin to "eliminate him".

Cocklecarrot: You mean he was going to poison his luncheon with polonium?

(Court erupts in sycophantic laughter at this example of judicial wit)

Hugefee: Ha, ha, ha, My Lord!

Cocklecarrot: Thank you, Sir Jonathan. But I see here that you and the other side have estimated that this hearing may well last for four years, with considerable costs for all parties. Could you please enlighten me as to how we are going to spin this one out for so long?

Hugefee: Indeed, My Lord. My learned friend and I have given a great deal of thought to this matter. I would therefore ask Your Lordship to consider the bundles of evidence numbered 1 to 4,812 which my learned friend and I have agreed should constitute the *res ipsissima* of the case.

Mr Cashinowicz: My Lord, my learned friend and I have also agreed a list of 6,812 witnesses, all of whose testimony is vital to the proper consideration by this court of the matters at issue. The list, as you will see, includes the names of the Russian prime minister, Mr Putin, the chief of the Russian security organisation Mr Igor Bumpovsky and various distinguished senior executives of the oil companies which were stolen from the Russian people in 1997 – I refer in particular to Mr Ripovsky, Mr Stealovich and Mr Krukhchev.

Cocklecarrot: I am indebted to you, Mr Cashinowicz. Your list of distinguished witnesses, many of whom will require the expensive services of interpreters, should go a long way to ensuring that we can all be sitting here until at least 2018. But now I suggest that this would be a suitable moment to adjourn for luncheon at the Garrick, where I gather that there is no risk of being served polonium with the potted shrimps.

(Court again collapses in hysterical laughter at this further prime example of the legendary humour of the Bench)

(The case continues)

"Is it that time already?"

STORM OF OUTRAGE OVER GADDAFI EXECUTION

by Our Legal Staff
Joshua Rosenbeard

THERE was worldwide condemnation yesterday of the brutal killing of Colonel Gaddafi before he could be brought before a properly constituted international court to answer for his crimes.

Thousands of lawyers from many countries protested at the way the "extra-judicial shooting" of the Libyan dictator had deprived them of the chance to take part in a trial which it had been predicted "could last for years".

Said one international lawyer last night, "Some of us are planning to bring a massive compensation claim against those responsible for this outrage, for cheating us out of the millions of pounds we could have earned in legal fees. Such an illegal slap in the face for the judicial process is truly a crime against humanity – or at least against the legal profession."

HSE Investigating Gaddafi Death

The Health & Safety Executive have reported that it is clear to them that proper guidelines "were not followed" during the capture and arrest of the Libyan leader. An interim report reveals: "There appeared to be a significant lack of defined roles amongst those who captured the Colonel which could have led to normal levels of arrest not being implemented properly. Also no one wore a hi-vis jacket or put on safety goggles before beating him and executing him at point-blank range."

GADDAFI
Is it right that we should show these photographs?

WORLDWIDE condemnation followed our publication of the graphic photos showing the killing of Libyan leader Colonel Gaddafi. The pictures are gruesome, graphic and grotesque – but are they also vital for an understanding of how newspapers need to boost circulation at a difficult time?

We are inviting you, as Daily Gnome readers, to judge for yourselves whether these are suitable pictures for public consumption or whether they are more suitable for a snuff movie or a new production of Marat/Sade by the RSC. *(Is this right? Ed.)*

In order to assist you to make an informed judgement on this vital issue we are publishing a 94-page special souvenir supplement with the most comprehensive selection of "Pre", "During" and "Post" death photos of Gaddafi ever seen.

Warning: Many readers may be deeply shocked at the £3 price of the supplement and we apologise if we have not published sufficient unpleasant photographs.

Now turn to p. 94 and see for yourself the really horrid one where the bullet goes in and all the blood gushes out. *(That's not **enough**! Ed.)*

Friday October 28, AD 30

Protestors Shut Down Temple – Money Lenders Continue As Normal

BY ST. MATTHEW PARRIS

A group of bearded idealists today occupied the great temple at the heart of the capital in protest at the worship of Mammon.

The occupation of the Temple has however prompted criticism from some observers who point out that it has had no effect whatsoever on the moneylenders but has shut down the one organisation that looks after the poor.

In The Courts

The Stephen Lawrence Case

Regina v Norris and Dobson

Justice Cocklecarrot: Ladies and gentlemen of the jury, it has been brought to my attention that a very grave contempt of court has been committed, *contemptualum magnatum*, which I am duty bound to draw to your attention and you are equally bound to put from your minds for ever.

I refer to an article by a Mr Rodwell Liddlejohn in a magazine known as the Spectator, which is a periodical devoted to the selling of luxury goods to the more affluent sections of society, including panama hats, fold-up walking sticks and similar items. Now, it may very well be that none of you are familiar with this periodical.

(Jury shake heads and look blank)

Cocklecarrot: No? Not even the musings of Charles Moore about his silk top hat?

(Jury still look vacant)

Cocklecarrot: So it may be that none of you has ever read Mr Liddlejohn who gives his opinion on a variety of topics every week, be it the undesirability of gypsies in your garden or the prospects of Millwall FC reaching the fourth round of the FA Cup. Nevertheless, it is the duty of the judge to inform you that Mr Liddlejohn is of the opinion that the accused are, in his own words, "guilty as hell" and "should be strung up forthwith, that being the only language they understand".

This is, of course, a gross contempt of this court and a disgraceful attempt to pervert the course of justice.

And now that you are fully acquainted with it, I ask you to banish it for ever from your minds and forget everything I have said.

Foreman: What was that, Your Honour?

Cocklecarrot: Excellent.

(The case continues)

The Eye Says

Rod Liddle is guilty of contempt. Forget the judge. Forget the jury. Just look at his record. Rod's a love rat who dumped his poor missus on their honeymoon and deserves to go to jail, along with the editor of the *Spectator* who is also clearly guilty. It's obvious. Enough said. Put them away. For ever.

The Alternative Rocky Horror Service Book

No. 94 A Service for the Closure of a Cathedral for Health and Safety Reasons.

The Canon *(for it is he)*: Brothers and Sisters, you are gathered here together in your tents to make your voices heard in protest at the recent failings of global capitalism.

Protestors: Yes indeedy!

The Canon: You are right welcome here as the church has a long tradition of helping the poor and crusading for social justice wheresoever it may be needful.

Protestors: Thanks be to you, O Canon.

(There then follows a reading from the Book of Health and Safety Regulations, Chapter 7, Page 75, paragraph 13b)

Reader: The erection of tented structures within 10 metres of the Cathedral's main access point creates an unacceptable safety hazard to visitors in so far as the tent guy ropes may cause serious injuries and the associated cooking devices of the camp dwellers may constitute a fire hazard to tourists and worshippers alike who are not covered by the ecclesiastical church insurance policies issued by Messrs Whittam Strobes of Chichester.

(The Dean will here take over and close the Cathedral doors until further notice)

The Dean: O Lord, close our doors.

Protestors: Result! Way to go!

The Dean: Let us now pray for the Cathedral and its revenues that are so severely stricken by this well-meaning but ultimately rather irritating protest. Let us pray for the gift shop with its agreeable postcards and reasonably priced audio guides which are now lying idle. Let us pray for the coffee shop with its excellent carrot cake and organic smoothies. And let us pray above all for those entrusted with collecting the admission fees which usually amount to over £16,000 per day.

Protestors *(outside)***:** Boo! Capitalist bastards!

The Dean: That is indeed a very fair comment, however, we are a business like many others with huge overheads and a small army of clergy whose modest stipends do need to be paid.

Clergy: Got any spare change, guv?

The Dean: We shall now sing our final hymn.

Hymn

*"There is a green hill far away
Perhaps you would like to go and
camp there instead"*

Protestors: We shall not be moved.

© CofE 2011

Nursery Times

Friday, October 28, 2011

OLD WOMAN URGED TO DOWNSIZE

by Our Housing Staff **Jack Built**

AN old woman who for years lived with a large number of children in a shoe has been criticised for remaining in the property despite the fact that the children have all grown up and left to claim benefits.

A leading charity, the Intergenerational Foundation, has demanded that elderly shoe dwellers should stop being so selfish and downsize for the benefit of the younger generation. A spokesman said, "What is she doing rattling around in that enormous shoe? She'd be much better off in a smaller slipper, or even a sock."

The old woman is however refusing to move. "The shoe is my home where I gave my children simple nutritious meals such as milk without any bread and then whipped them all soundly before they were taken into care by Nurseryland Social Services."

ON OTHER PAGES
● *Jemima Puddleduck joins New Statesman p. 2* ● *Fantastic Mr. Fox resigns p. 3* ● *Badger not gassed by Toad p. 94*

Britain's Recession Booming

FIGURES from the Office of National Statistics showing growth of 0.5 percent in the past three months have confirmed that Britain is caught in the grip of a recessionary boom.

"Things have never been worse out there on the High Street and that's why we're seeing such strong recessionary growth figures," said one economist wearing a grey suit.

"Things have never been worse out there on the High Street and that's why we're seeing such strong recessionary growth figures," said another economist wearing a grey suit, who might actually have been the same economist but we're not sure as they all look alike.

Church Split Over Camp Protest

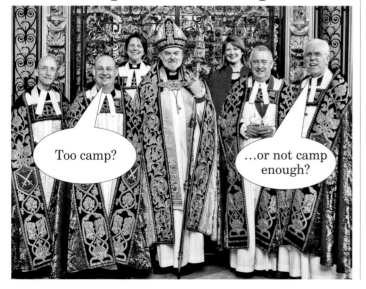

Too camp?

...or not camp enough?

What Will Rebekah's Baby Be Called?

As a mark of respect for the privacy of the former Editor of the News of the World, the Eye is asking its readers to choose a sensitive name for her unborn surrogate child.

Boy	Girl
Rupert	Rupertella
James	Wendi
Sky	Elizabeth
Sunny	Paige (3)
Cameron	Papparazza
Chipping	Mulcaria
Norton	Wappinga
Jeremy Clarkson	Sarah Brown

(That's enough names)

(AND PETROL CAN)

Satirical Magazine Doesn't Put Mohammed On Cover — Offices Not Firebombed

by **Charlie Hebdo**

London, Monday

The controversial British magazine *Private Eye* failed to put an image of the prophet on its front pages in its latest issue and, as a direct result, was not burned to the ground immediately.

Said the editor, "It was an act of some courage to make this decision, but I thought it would be much braver to attack the Church of England instead".

NIALL FERGUSON,
the Laurence A. Tosch Professor of Advanced Money Studies at Harvard

Professor, do you have a favourite spoon?

That's typical of the British press, focussing on trivial details of my private life, when I am the world's greatest living historian.

Would you say that spoons have played an important part in your career as the world's greatest living historian?

Oh, I can't wait to get out of this pathetic country, Britain. All you people can do is to go on about spoons, when some of the world's most important books have been written by me.

Have you ever referred to spoons in any of your very important books?

OK, so I've left my wife for a very beautiful and very clever younger woman. Can't you just give it a rest?

Has anything amusing ever happened to you in connection with a spoon?

You keep coming back to these bloody spoons. What's the f****ng matter with you British journalists? Just because I'm the best-looking guy in the world and the cleverest, doesn't mean I've got to sit here answering your bloody stupid questions about spoons.

Thank you very much, Professor Ferguson, and good luck with your marvellous new book 'The Life And Times of Financier Sir Fred Goodwin'.

NEXT WEEK: *Simon Schama, "Me and My Shaman".*

"…and this is our top-of-the-range model"

Does this picture reveal the big news that we've all suspected?

DOES this incredible picture of Kate's hand hovering vaguely near her stomach prove once and for all what some of us have guessed all along? **Yes**! It provides conclusive evidence that we are utterly desperate to put in pictures of Kate Middleton and will print anything with her in it to fill space.

ON OTHER PAGES ● *Kate and Wills' new apartment in Kensington Palace – will this fill up some more space? Yes.* **4**

That New Female Royal Line Of Succession In Full

1. Kate Middleton
2. The Rt. Hon. Lady Grantham of Downton
3. Kim Kardashian
4. Joanna Lumley
5. Lady Mary Crawley
6. Pippa's left cheek
7. Pippa's right cheek (to act as consort)
8. Ann Widdecombe
9. Nancy Dell'Olio

(Quite enough. Ed.)

Only in the Eye

Renowned Arse Expert Was Secret Lover Of Paintings
by Our Arse Correspondent the late **Sir Anthony Very-Blunt**

IN A sensational memoir the country's leading arse expert, Brian R. Sewell, revealed that he has long been a private connoisseur of old masters, regularly haunting art galleries and prowling around auction houses in the hope of "picking up" drawings and other artworks "on the cheap".

Says Sewell, "I must have seen thousands of pictures in my time but I am not ashamed of it.

"Some days I may have *done* three or four galleries before breakfast and fitted in a quickie round the Royal Academy before lunch.

"But that was how it was."

He continued, "I would have preferred to be a Catholic priest, but instead I devoted myself to the seedy, shadowy world of full-time art appreciation."

The Boris Johnson Book of London

by London Mayor **BORIS JOHNSON**

Chapter 94:
The True Story of Dick Whittington

EVERYONE thinks they know the story of Dick Whittington, as we see it in the jolly old Christmas panto. But the true story is a damn sight more interesting, what!

Right. Once upon a time there was this very bright young lad with a mop of blond hair who went to Eton and Oxford, but then decided to travel up to London to seek his fame and fortune.

Someone had told him that the streets of London were "paved with women". To which Dick replied, "Cripes, I can't wait."

So off he set with nothing but a humble knapsack over his shoulder and a slim volume of Latin poetry to wile away the long hours of his journey.

But on arrival in the capital, Dick found life very hard. The only job he could get was a humble editorship of the *Spectator*.

But before long he was fired even from this lowly position, and he despaired that his grand dreams would ever come true.

Sadly, he decided to leave London. But, as he pedalled up Highgate Hill, he heard the ringing of his mobile phone.

It was his old schoolfriend from long ago, Dave. "Turn again", said the voice, "You will be Lord Mayor of London, because we haven't got anyone else."

Overjoyed, Dick returned and within days was proclaimed Mayor of London, exactly as the mobile had foretold.

He had defeated the hated King Newt, to the delight of all men and women of London, but particularly the women.

And from that moment on Dick became the most popular man in the nation on account of his roguish ways, gift for witty public speaking and deep knowledge of classical literature.

No wonder that before long the deeply unpopular prime minister of the day, Dave, was forced to step down as the people of England demanded that Boris (as Dick was now known) should become their rightful king.

Tomorrow: The Blitz. How Sir Winston Johnson rallied Londoners in their darkest hour with his legendary speech, "We shall fight Johnny Hun on the beaches and all that kind of stuff, dontcha know."

HOW EUROPE HAS AGED CAMERON

2010   2011

BILL CLINTON SENDS PICTURE MESSAGE TO WRONG WOMAN

IS DAWN WORRYINGLY THIN?

By Our Health Staff
Clare Monger

FOR YEARS Dawn French was the roly-poly comedienne who became an 18-stone national treasure by showing us she wasn't embarrassed by her voluptuous natural curves.

We at the Mail demonstrated just how much we loved her by running sympathetic pieces such as, "Dawn French: is She Too Fat?", "What Sort of Roly-Poly Model Do You Think You Are, Fatso?" and "Fatty French Causes House Prices to Fall by Being So Fat".

Yet now Dawn has gone on the diet we always suggested she needed and has become a svelte, slinky, skeletal shadow of her former self, prompting fears for her health.

Friends, who we have just made up, tell us that the new thin Dawn is wasting away, causing alarm about possible anorexia.

Doctors, who we have also just made up, are voicing concerns that the strain on the newly thin Dawn's heart may be too much even though they said the same thing when she was fat (or would have done if they hadn't been made up).

The fictitious doctors added that the stick-insect-like Dawn may well suffer skin complaints, depression and almost certain death if she doesn't eat anything ever again.

Worse still, a business analyst (who as you may have guessed is not entirely unfictitious) told us, "Since Dawn's irresponsible crash weight loss, national chocolate sales have plummeted causing a crisis of economic confidence which has led the housing market to collapse completely."

On Other Pages ● **Nigella**: For God's sake, put some weight back on so we can say you're too fat and you should lose some weight, you great big, bloated, burquini bimbo! **2** ● **Kate**: For God's sake, lose some weight, your Highness, so we can say you're too thin and not as attractive as your sister with the big arse **3** ● PLUS **Femail**: Why are women so self-conscious about their bodies? **94**

POLLY FILLER

Half-term Nightmare

THE drive back from our holiday home in Pol Roger in Cornwall to Primrose Hell(!) should take seven hours. But last week, at the end of half-term, it took longer than the Retreat from Moscow, the Jarrow March and Captain Scott's Expedition to the South Pole, all rolled into one! And made all of them look like a teddybears' picnic!

Picture the scene in the Fillermobile as it crawled along the motorway with toddler Charlie screaming in the back before being sick into his new Captain Haddock rucksack (talk about blistering typhoons of vomit!) because he had eaten a giant Snail Porridge Happy Meal at the Heston Blumenthal Little Chef outside Newport Pagnall. Yes, I know it's not on the way – blame the new Jeremy Clarkson SatNav, which the Useless Simon insisted on installing after he had seen it plugged at the Live Top Gear Gadget Show at the Reading Hexagon, presented by the Stig, with a special video link to James May... Where was I?...

Honestly, cooped up in a tin box smelling of regurgitated Blumenthal Burger for 12 hours with a distressed child endlessly asking "Are we there yet?" between persistent projectile pukes is surely any woman's idea of hell?!

No wonder the au pair was hysterical by the time they finally arrived in London. And thank goodness I sensibly flew back from Newquay, thus avoiding all those ghastly middle-class people with holiday homes clogging up the roads with their smelly 4x4s full of spoilt, nauseous infants!

For some unknown reason, when I asked the au pair to disinifect the car seat, the annoying Wee Pee handed in her notice, saying she would rather go back to her village in Thailand. I told her not to be silly because it's all been washed away in the floods.

Really! Then the drippy girl dissolved into floods herself – of tears!

If anyone has had a worse half-term than that, don't let me know!

© Polly Filler 2011.

A Doctor Writes

AS A doctor, I'm often asked, "Is alcohol too cheap?".

The simple answer is "Yesh!". What happens is that the doctor gets depressed by the number of his patients who drink too much and sees Tesco is offering 3 for 2 on litre bottles of vodka. He buys the vodka, drinks it and then experiences temporary feelings of well-being or *medicalis alcoholicensis normalis*, to give it the full scientific name.

However, there are some side effects associated with this condition, including headaches, nausea, trembling, short-term memory loss, headaches, nausea, trembling and... where was I? Indeed, where am I? Oh no, I've fallen asleep in the park and I'm meant to be at my surgery! I'll just pop into Lidl on the way for some of their very reasonably priced own-brand window cleaner.

If you are worried about cheap alcohol, you should avoid Waitrose at all costs.

© A Doctor, 2011.

"You're married, aren't you?"

PERCIVAL

SHOCK HUMAN RIGHTS COURT VERDICT

by Our Legal Staff **Joshua Rosenkavalier**

IN A landmark ruling yesterday, the European Court of Human Rights found that Mr Abu al Qaeda had a basic human right to remain in Britain in order to exercise his profession as a world-class terrorist.

The court found that the British government had been quite wrong in attempting to deport Mr al Qaeda to Jordan on the grounds he couldn't possibly receive a fair trial because he had attempted to blow up large numbers of people in that country, not to mention various other parts of the world.

The 47 judges rejected the British government's argument that a Palestinian who comes into your country on a forged passport and plans terrorist outrages should perhaps be sent home to his own country.

The judges described this argument as totally unacceptable and found that Britain had further infringed Mr al Qaeda's rights by keeping him in prison where he was unable to practise his profession.

They further found that the government must pay Mr al Qaeda's family "substantial benefits" as compensation for the fact that he is unable to support them through his work as an international terrorist.

Mr al Qaeda's QC, Ms Deirdre Spart, asked the court, "What torture will the British government come up with next for my client? No doubt they will expect him to work in Poundland, stacking shelves, when he could be using his exceptional talents to murder very large numbers of people."

SYRIA LATEST

See? No blood on them…

Timetable agreed for UN intervention in Syria

AUSTERITY 'WILL LEAD TO AUSTERITY', SAY ECONOMISTS

THERE was widespread shock today after the leading economist think-tank, the IBO (The Institute for the Bleeding Obvious), claimed that the Government's austerity measures would lead to an era of austerity in Britain.

"We've calculated that the result of slashing Government spending and sacking loads of people," said a boring man in spectacles, "is that Government spending reduces significantly and the number of unemployed people increases rapidly.

"From these findings we've drawn the conclusion that austerity measures will lead to austerity."

The Chancellor was quick to reject the findings, saying everyone he knows has just been awarded six-figure bonuses by the bank they work for, so happy days were here again.

(Reuters)

I AM PRACTISING PAY RESTRAINT

I MAY NEED MORE PRACTICE… MASSIVE BONUS

INDIA AID – ROW GROWS

by Our Development Staff **Rupee Murdoch**

THE controversy over "Indian Aid" escalated yesterday when ministers called upon the government "to do more for third world countries, like Britain".

Said the Indian Finance Minister, Mahatma Handout, "India is a very wealthy country with a very strong economy and it is shameful that we give so little to the desperate people in England.

"It is very easy to say that they waste their money on defence projects instead of spending it on health, but we all know that the infrastructure is falling apart and the small wealthy elite do nothing to help the massive underclass – the so-called 'unworkables'."

The minister concluded, "India must live up to its post-colonial responsibility and start sending aid packages to the poor and needy of Britain at once."

POLLY FILLER

on the latest parenting book *French Children Don't Throw Food* by Pouilly Fillere

IF I read another piece telling me how great French women are at bringing up children, I think **I** shall throw food at someone! And that someone will be Ms Oh-so-perfect Fillère with her immaculate hairdo, elegant skinny jeans and wonderful toddlers who sleep through the night and happily sit through family meals without misbehaving!

Well, let's set the record straight, Pouilly, whoever you are, we British working women, juggling careers and motherhood on the tightrope of the modern career/lifestyle balance, are doing a pretty good job raising children, thank you very much, without **your** Gallic two Euros worth!

Let's be honest, it's no wonder your children are so docile when you keep them up all night at the dinner table and drug them with red wine from the age of six months until they fall asleep on the tablecloth, just so that you and your useless partner, Simone, can wear berets and smoke Gauloises into the early hours, arguing about the Extreme Philosophy programme on Canal Plus X+ Un, presented by Jacques Mai…

For your information, Pouilly, I've done a very good job of raising my toddler, Charlie, who is well-mannered, disciplined, tidy and polite.

Just ask our au-pair, Françoise, whom I was sensible enough to bring over from Lille and employ to look after Charlie 24/7 whilst I write my hilarious best-selling new book *English Children Don't Throw Up (except on long car journeys to Cornwall at half-term!)*, Pearson, Johnson and Cavendish, £19.99.

© Polly Filler 2012.

Phil Space talks to the star of War Horse

Phil: So, Joey, what was it like working with Spielberg?

Joey: Well, it's every horse's dream to work with Steven and when the call came from Los Angeles, I nearly keeled over with shock. Me, a virtual unknown... working with the director of "Jaws".

Phil: Oh, come on, you're one of the top horses in your field!

Joey: Bless you! But, no, I thought it was my old mate Saucy Ned winding me up.

Phil: And how was the experience of the film?

Joey: I have to say, Steven was just marvellous – kind, modest, thoughtful and very generous with the sugar lumps. He really knows how to get the best out of a horse. It was a privilege.

Phil: Did you do your own stunts?

Joey: Oh, yes, I insisted on that. I spent months learning to be ridden and that really helped

me get into the part.

Phil: How were the rest of the cast?

Joey *(laughs)*: They say you should never work with children or humans, but really, they were very well behaved and I didn't feel upstaged at all. Emily was a sweetie, Benedict's a trooper, well, not literally – he's playing a cavalry officer, but you know what I mean... oh, and it's such a wonderful script by lovely Richard Curtis and lovely Lee Hall and lovely...

Phil: So, how are you coping with the fame?

Joey: It's important not to get too big-headed, but then that's difficult when you're a horse.

Phil: And what next for Joey?

Joey: It's very exciting, Phil. My agent tells me he has got me a starring role in a glue commercial.

Phil: Break a leg!

● *War Horse is on every page of every newspaper until you admit defeat and go and see it.*

St Cake's Boys Star in Top Film and TV Roles

by Our Showbiz Staff **Lunchtime O.E.**

WITH their high cheekbones, cut-glass accents and natural public-school confidence, the posh boys of St Cake's are taking over our screens. If the part needs a stiff upper lip, a plummy voice and an ability to wear white tie and tails, it is to the independent, fee-paying Midlands school for boys that casting directors immediately turn.

Here are just some of the old Cakeians wowing us at the moment:

★ **Caspian 'Floppy' Hare** (21) in the Hollywood blockbuster *Bird Horse*, playing tragic First World War officer Lieutenant Floppy 'Hare' Caspian.

★ **Clovis St John Poshington** (22) in the upcoming BBC drama *Horsesong*, adapted from the novel *War and Sex* by famous old Cakeian novelist Ford Cortina Ford, playing the lovesick hero John St Clovis Poshworth.

★ **Jolyon Goodchap** (27) who plays Captain Jolyon Goodchap, who is a thoroughly good chap, in the forthcoming 94-part HBO WWI mini-series *Songbirds on Parade*.

St Cake's Head of Drama, Emily Fruitington-Fruit, says the high-profile domination of the airwaves by Cake's boys is no coincidence.

"We do special drama classes here in staring moodily straight ahead, not saying anything for long periods and walking about looking upper-class."

She continued, "Once the boys have mastered these skills, then there really is no stopping them. The Sky is the limit – but obviously BBC is better."

But there are those who are unhappy that these sons of privilege are getting all the top parts, playing sons of privilege, at a time when acting jobs are hard to come by.

"It's unfair," said one furious critic. "Even the job of Prime Minister has been given to an old Cakeian. Just because he vaguely looks the part and remembers his lines, he has taken the plummy role."

Mr Ed Miliband – for it was he – then added, "It's time more state-educated boys were allowed to dress up in white tie and tails and have a go."

However, the Headmaster, Mr Kipling, refused to be embarrassed by the success of his thespian alumni.

"We make exceedingly good Cakeians," he told parents at the annual school production *All Go On The West End Front* by Sir Terence Stoppagan (OC).

Star of The Artist: Oscar Acceptance Speech in Full

Jimmy Wales Defends Wikipedia Black-Out

WIKIPEDIA founder, Jimmy Wales, has defended blacking out Wikipedia for one day in protest at new US anti-piracy legislation.

"I see myself as defending a point of principle, just like Martin Luther King had to do during the Alamo.

"He and his redcoats refused to give way to Hitler and, if it wasn't for his brave stand, we wouldn't have the trouser press. And I think that says it all really."

Jimmy Wales is 104.

That Antony Worrall Thompson Menu In Full

Salad Nickoise

– ❋ –

Beefburglars

– ❋ –

Fish Light-fingers

– ❋ –

Cheese Stuffed in Jacket

– ❋ –

Collar of Lamb

– ❋ –

Stollen

– ❋ –

Porridge

– ❋ –

Served with Ginger Beard and Tea (leaf) or Innocent-until-proven-guilty Smoothie

---

NORTH KOREAN WAR HORSE OPENS

And now I eat horse

"One day, son, all this will be yours"

£1 TRILLION NATIONAL DEBT

LAWRENCE MURDERERS CONVICTED

Huge rise in house prices

by **Paul Dacresofthisstuff**

THANKS to the Daily Mail's fearless campaign, the price of your house has *(cont. 94)*

HOW WE ENDED SLAVERY

Pages: 1, 2, 3, 4-94

"Rejoice now that colonialism is dead"
Editorial by William Dacreforce

CENTRE PAGES: The stars remember their favourite toys from childhood

---

SHAVING BAN   RAYBAN   TALIBAN

'U.S. OCCUPATION OF AMERICA IS FAILURE' DECLARE CRITICS

AFTER a 250-year military presence, the achievements of the American occupation of America have been called sharply into question. "Despite spending billions of dollars, the country still remains a hotbed of gun-toting religious extremists with only a toehold on democracy," say critics. "Pity the ordinary American people. At least in Iraq they were only there for 8 years. This looks like going on forever." *(Reuters)*

A message from the Mayor of London

Boris Johnson

Cripes! I expect you've heard about my new baby – but hold your horses – this time I'm not referring to yours truly being caught with his trousers down and getting some totty up the duff! No, Bozza has been as good as gold (this week!) and Percy Pecker is well and truly grounded, if you know what I mean.

So – where was I? Oh yes, Boris's new baby. It's going to be noisy, smelly and keep everyone awake at night – yes, it's an airport! And not just any old airport, it's an airport in the middle of a river! Classic, eh?

The boffins tell me that Boris Island is a corker of an idea – flying Johnny foreigner and his missus into jolly old Blighty in their millions to unload all their oodles of dosh into our waiting pockets.

Ergo – UK plc will turn a handsome profit, which will easily pay for the few billions we had to shell out on the new-fangled aerodrome chap.

Makes perfect sense. And it's a win-win situation. I win as Mayor. And then I become Prime Minister.

No offence to Dozy Dave who is doing sterling work annoying the frogs and square-heads, but if only he had this sort of Boris-style vision he wouldn't look so much of a chump!

Toodle pip!

Boris

PS. Forgot to mention the other big plus about dumping a double-sized Heathrow right on Father Thames. Plane-loads of fruity stewardesses jetting in and needing a night out with someone who can show them a good time. Crikey! Down Percy!

GLENDA SLAGG

Fleet Street's Right Royal Writer (Geddit?!)

■ **SO KATE MIDDLETON is 30?** So what? Some of us have been 30 for years and we don't go on and on and on about it?!! What's the big deal?! OK, so she'll have some kids, she'll let herself go, and before she knows it we'll all be asking if she's too fat?!? Glenda's advice to you, dearie, is enjoy yourself while you still can – it's all downhill from here to overweighty Katie (Geddit!!?!)

■ THE DUCHESS of Cambridge is 30!! And she doesn't look a day over 29!!?! With a figure to Di for (geddit!?!), a prince on her arm and a bun in the oven (probably) she glows like the candles on her birthday cake!!?! But take a tip from Auntie Glenda, your royal loveliness, don't eat the cake for Gawd's sake or you'll begin the long downward spiral from Flirty Thirty to Flabby Forty and Fatso Fifty!!?! (*You've done this bit, Ed.*)

■ **THE COUNTESS of Wessex –** what a disgrace!?!! Taking blood-soaked baubles from the Butcher of Bahrain!? Shame on you, Sponger Sophie, for jettin' off round the world fillin' your wheelie suitcase with tyrant's trinkets!?! Time to flog them – and I don't mean the Brave Bahrani protesters, Ma'am, or should that be Sma'am!?!!

■ TIARAS OFF to Savvy Sophie Wessex!! At last there's one royal who is making a profit rather than a-loungin' and a-scroungin' off the state!!?! Why shouldn't a gal pick up a few baubles for her trouble, especially when hopeless hubby Edward can't keep her in the style to which she's accustomed??! Go for it, Wessex Girl!!?!

■ **SEEN THE Madonna film about Edward and Mrs Simpson?!! It's all about an American floozy on the make who the beastly Brits all hate!!? And I don't mean Wallis do I, Madonna??! Get over it, your Madge – you're no longer the Queen of Pop. You've abdicated to make way for Lady Gaga!!?! Now there's real Rock 'n' Roll Royalty!!? (*Geddit!!??*)**

■ HERE THEY ARE – Glenda's January Males (*Geddit?!?!*)

● **Professor Stephen Hawking!?!!** So you think women are a mystery, do you?? Well, why don't you come round to my place for some Big Bang Theory!!?!

● **Michael Morpurgo!?!!** He's Mr Warhorse and the former Children's Laureate, stoopid?!! Mmmm Michael??! If you fancy a gallop I wouldn't say 'neigh'!!?!

● **Jacob Gedleyihlekisa Zuma!?!!** Crazy name, crazy president of South Africa!?!!

Byeee!!

Lines on the Wish of Mr Alex Salmond to hold a Referendum on Whether Scotland Should be Freed from the Oppressive Yoke of the Hated English

By WILLIAM REES-MCGONAGALL

There was no question in the year two thousand and twelve
That far back in history you would have to delve
To find any Scottish leader of such brave determination
As the one who wished to see Scotland as again an
                  independent nation.
Alex Salmond was this Braveheart's name
Not since William Wallace had any Scot won such fame
Suddenly there he was on every TV show
Proclaiming, "The moment has come for Scotland to go".
"In 2014," he said, "we'll let the Scottish people choose.
At last we will free them to express their views.
Seven hundred years after the English at Bannockburn were
                  slain
I shall give the Scots the chance to do it again."
The canny Alex was careful not to pick the year before
Because this might have reminded the Scots of another war.
This was in 1513 when at the battle of Flodden
The field with Scottish, not English, blood was sodden.
At Alex's bold move the Sassenach leaders were aghast.
They were fearful that the Union might soon be a thing of
                  the past.
Scotland would soon become a nation all on its own
Having kicked out the English and the Queen off her throne.
Free to join Europe and to keep all their oil
How their proud boasts would make English blood boil!
But then poor Alex suffers a terrible blow
When he sees what opinion polls both north and south show:
In Scotland a majority reject his great plan,
Whereas the English want the Scots to leave as fast as they can.
This was not what puir wee Alex had in mind at all
It seemed the wrong nation had answered his call
So he quickly came up with a brilliant new scheme
As the only way he could realise at least most of his dream.
To the West Lothian question he had at last find a solution
And the name of his answer was 'Maximum Devolution'.
Everyone would surely vote for 'Devo Max'
Allowing Alex to rule Scotland but paid for out of English tax.

© W. Rees-McGonagall

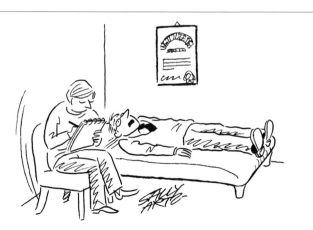

"Eventually, I stopped trying to gain my parents' approval, and started trying to gain my children's approval"

'CREW LEFT SHIP BEFORE US'
Rats' Shock Claim

by Our Shipping Staff
Lloyd Listing

A **NUMBER** of furious rats today criticised the crew of the sunken ship, the Costa Lotalives, for deserting the stricken vessel even before it started sinking.

Said one angry rodent, "I was thinking about jumping ship when I was barged out of the way by the captain.

"He was shouting 'Women and children last'," continued the rat, who had been enjoying the holiday of a lifetime on board the giant disaster waiting to happen *(surely "luxury cruise ship"?)*.

Lawyers for the captain later, however, issued a statement denying the rats' claims.

Excuse Hits Rocks

"Captain Shittino was bravely standing on the bridge when he slipped over, fell through the door and down the corridor onto the deck then up a ladder into the lifeboat which he inadvertently launched and sailed off, thus leaving all the rats behind.

"It is an unfortunate set of coincidences, but I am sure you agree it could have happened to no one."

Cartoonists Go Overboard As Huge Metaphor Hits Newspapers

by Steve 'Lutine' Bell

THERE were scenes of pandemonium today as cartoonists scrambled over each other to be the first to draw the capsized cruise liner representing the Italian government, the British Conservative/Liberal Coalition or the Euro currency.

Man Over Drawingboard!

Onlookers said, "It was a political cartoon just waiting to happen. It was every man for himself."

Not since the Titanic has a ship gone down so well with cartoonists who *(We get the idea. Ed.)*

Cruise Tragedy: Fruity Girl Barely Escapes

A fruity Moldovan girl seen dining with the Captain just moments before the Costa Concordia's fatal accident has told of her escape from the ship. For details, see our photo supplement, "The Fruity Girl Stood on the Burning Deck",

available for just £2.99.

On other pages

● More pics of that fruity girl... **2-5**
● Fruity Dutch sixteen-year-old sails around the world... **6** ● Several less photogenic people drown... **94**

SHOCK NEW PAUL BURRELL ADMISSION

I didn't just help myself to Diana's jewels...

...I took Fergie's make-up as well

Those **Paul Johnson** Desvert Island Discs In Full

Spank You For The Music – Abba
Red Cheeks In The Sunset – Connie Francis
Family Affair – Sly And The Family Values ♫
Wives And Lovers – Randy Williams ♪
Smack My Bitch Up – The Prodigy ♫
Gloria – Van Morrison ♪
Secret Love – Doris Day ♪
The Old Cane Bottom Chair – George Formby ♪
Do As I Say Not As I Do – Ed Harcourt

Luxury item: A nice comfy cushion

NEVER TOO OLD

A new love story by Dame Sylvie Krin, author of
Heir of Sorrows and *Duchess of Hearts*

THE STORY SO FAR: Octogenarian media mogul Rupert Murdoch is being encouraged to use the new social media by his young bride, Wendi. Now read on...

RUPERT's elderly fingers fumbled as he tried to tap out a message on the tiny keys of his new Conrad Blackberry mobile phone, a Christmas present from his beautiful bride from the land of the prawn cracker.

"Jeez, Wendi! This thing's smaller than a Koala's didgeridoo on a cold night in Kookaburra Creek."

He squinted at the screen through his Pierre Moron designer spectacles, hoping for some soothing words of sympathy, but none came.

"You twitter, Lupert! You show world you not senile old man who let Dim Sun ruin everything!" cried Wendi.

And with an elegant pirouette and reverse kick, the agile martial arts expert decapitated the stuffed mannequin labelled "Tom Watson MP" that had been Rupert's surprise Christmas present to *her*.

"Strewth, Wend! I don't know what I'm bloody doing here. Am I tweeting or retweeting or what?"

"At moment, you taking picture of floor!" Wendi exclaimed in frustration. Then suddenly the phone burst into life, playing the opening bars of the hit novelty record "Grandad", re-recorded specially for Rupert by the Digger's Creek Symphonia and Chorus, one of Australia's premier classical ensembles.

"No, Lupert! Now you change ling tone. Go back to twittering!"

The elderly tycoon sighed as he punched more buttons. If only his former flame-haired chief executive were here. Rebekah was always so good at the new technology.

"Couldn't I get Bekky to do this bollocks for me? I'm paying her enough to sit around on her arse doing diddly squat."

"We no talk about Lebekah in this house!!" The icy stare of the dragon lady could have frozen a sausage on a Bondi Beach barbie.

"You concentrate on sending tweet, Lupert. You tell forrowers how you having nice cup of cocoa."

"Alright, alright, my little rice noodle. I'm on the case." A chastened Rupert concentrated once again on the digital device and addressed the mini keyboard.

Was this right? Was he following or being followed? What did it all mean? The Twittersphere would surely expect global insights from a man of his international stature, not just something about drinking cocoa.

Perhaps he should write a tribute to his new friend and Republican presidential candidate, Dick Sanatorium – was that how you spelt it? His confidence began to wane...

Then suddenly the speakerphone activated and a familiar voice rang out across the New York penthouse suite on the 94th floor of the Evilempire State Building.

"Hi. This is Hugh Grant. You're through to my voicemail. Just, er, you know, er, leave me a message. Fuckety, fuckety fuck! *Beeeeep!*"

Rupert's blood froze and in the ensuing silence across the city a police siren wailed.

(To be continued)

THE EYE'S MOST READ STORIES

Climate Change Conference Agrees to Hold Another Climate Change Conference

There was joy amongst delegates at the International Climate Change Conference as a last minute deal was reached to hold another climate change conference in four years' time.

"Right up to the last minute there were fears that our governments could grumble what a total waste of time these conferences are," said one delegate, "but this deal secured my place at this luxurious hotel for the foreseeable future."

Jubilant environmentalists then flew home to tell everyone they were going to fly right back again.

Elderly Care Reforms 'Shelved Till They're Dead'

A government plan to shake up the care of the elderly will now be put off to a more "realistic time frame" – ie, when they are all dead, as the Treasury is believed to be reluctant to agree to the extra money needed *(cont p. 94)*

A Doctor Writes

A lot of people in my surgery ask me, "Doctor, why are you feeling my breasts?".

I inform them that, following the scare over breast implants made with industrial silicon, there is a medical need to monitor all implants to make sure there isn't an imminent danger of rupturing.

"But Doctor," they invariably reply, "I don't have breast implants."

This is inevitably followed by a short period of hysterical screaming, which I generally treat by pouring myself a stiff Scotch to calm myself down.

I will then refer myself to a good lawyer in the hope that my long-term prognosis for being struck off isn't as bad as the papers make out. © *A Doctor.*

JANUARY SALES OFF TO FLYING START

By Our Retail Correspondent **Janet High-Street-Portas**

THERE were scenes of pandemonium outside Conservative Central Office yesterday as bargain hunters fought to be first through the doors at Smith Square to get their hands on the amazing deals on offer.

Hedge fund tycoons and leading industrialists waved their cheque books frantically as they grabbed the cut-price honours on sale.

Said one, "I've been queuing for months for this. I had my heart set on a knighthood and I've got one!"

SELL OUT

Said another, "I can't believe it. I got a lovely title and it was reduced from £500,000 to just £200,000."

The manager, Mr Cameron, was "delighted" by the response to the sale.

"People say that there is no money around and that the public are not willing to spend any of their hard-earned cash. Our January sale proves that they are wrong and if you are offering the right goods at the right price then you can still attract the punters."

Critics, however, were quick to pour cold water on the sale. Said Mr Miliband, "They are flogging off rubbish cheap to gullible idiots and derailing the whole honours system. We would do it much better."

DRAWING ALL FAITHS TOGETHER

Hi!

And can I wish all of you in all your faith communities around the world a belated "Happy Holiday", whether your holy day was Christmas, Hanukkah, Eid, Diwali, Saturnalia, the birth of L. Ron Hubbard, the Jedi Festival of Light Sabres, the pagan feast of Wiccapedia, or whatever.

As you know, we at DAFT celebrate the whole family of faiths, all of us believers in the mystery at the heart of life.

And, d'you know what is still the greatest mystery of all? Just how much money I have made in the last year!

But, y'know, even with all my thoughts and meditations on the subject, I am not sure that **I** know the answer to this!

And perhaps some things on earth are best left unknown, "invisible", "God-only-wise". As I used to say when I was just a humble vicar of St Albion's, "We must count our blessings, but we don't have to publish them all!"

Yours,

Rev. T. Blair

Chief Executive, D.A.F.T.

(former vicar of St Albion's)

This painting's like really iconic. BIRCH

Letter to the Editor

Names of the year

Sir, As is customary at this time of year, I have compiled a list of the most popular names recorded in your births and deaths announcements over the past 12 months (last year's position in brackets).

Boys	Girls
1. Fenton (-)	Vajazzle (-)
2. Jesus Christ (-)	Dellolio (-)
3. Wills (1)	Kate (1)
4. Harry (2)	Pippa (-)
5. Pip (6)	PIP (-)
6. Sherlock (-)	Alesha (7)
7. Suarez (9)	Towie (4)
8. Mitt (-)	Zumba (3)
9. Kim Jong (-)	Meryl (-)
10. Sir Peregrine Worsthorne (9)	Maggie (-)

Yours faithfully

THE RT. REV. AHMED SACHS-COBURG, Suffragan Bishop of the Falkland Islands and Associated Dependencies.

"Don't forget – if anyone asks, you've always lived within the School of Athens catchment area"

25

'WE'LL BORROW OUR WAY OUT OF DEBT'

Chancellor's shock pledge

by Our Economics Staff **Stephanie Flounders and Robert Pest**

A CONFIDENT George Osborne yesterday pledged that in order to end the public deficit, he would borrow a further £500 billion.

To the cheers of Tory backbenchers, the Chancellor said, "Reducing the national debt is our top priority and I will not be deflected from this course, even if it means that we have to borrow a sum equivalent to our entire GDP every week."

Mr Osborne was immediately attacked by Shadow Chancellor Ed Balls, who said, "That was our idea. The Chancellor has just chosen to steal our Labour policy of massive and reckless borrowing – what is he going to announce next, a huge public spending programme on infrastructure projects?"

To Labour cheers, Mr Osborne immediately stood up to announce a huge public spending programme on infrastructure programmes. "We're going to spend our way out of debt," he told weeping Tory backbenchers, listing his top five projects to be launched by 2009.

These include:

● extension of the M25 to 50 lanes in both directions, incorporating a new "aero-hub" replacement for Heathrow on the site of the former Little Chef at Junction 94

● new 300mph high speed railway to link Land's End with John O'Groats, cutting journey time by 23 minutes

● the closure of all remaining manufacturing plants to replace them with Enterprise Zones, co-funded by the People's Republic of China Central Bank, the Qatari Sovereign Wealth Fund and the Treasury, thanks to a loan from the Bank of Greece

● a £10 billion investment in British technology to find a cure for serious animal diseases, such as cat flu, depression in dogs and Piscine Alzheimer's with particular reference to domestic goldfish

● a £2 million project based at the former Battersea Power Station to extract sunbeams from cucumbers as an alternative energy source to nuclear power stations.

© Dr J. Swift, 1726
(That's enough Osborne, Ed.)

WHAT NEXT AFTER MOVEMBER?

The Eye suggests more fundraising fun with a calendar theme to follow up the hugely successful month of moustache mania!

● **ANTANDDECEMBER**
DRESS up like your favourite Geordie TV presenters and make your friends eat a bucket of maggots – for charity!

● **TANUARY**
BANISH the winter blues by topping up your tan (real or fake), whilst raising money for a worthy cause.

● **FEZBRUARY**
WEAR a fez to work and help your favourite under-resourced local or national charity.

● **MARRCH**
IMPERSONATE TV's top inquisitor Andrew Marr and take out a sponsored superinjunction so no one can find out why you are doing it!!

● **APERIL**
LET ALL your body hair grow until you resemble our simian ancestors – go Ape-ril in a good cause!

● **MAY**
WEAR a flowery blouse and become Jeremy Clarkson's sidekick James May or maybe build a life-size Lego Great Wall of China using *(That's enough charity, Ed.)*

Friday, November 25, 2011

CHICKEN MERVYN PREDICTS SKY TO FALL ON HEAD

by Our Financial Staff **Crystal Ball**

THE well-known economic forecaster and Governor of the Bank of Toyland, Chicken Mervyn, today ran around shouting wildly, "We're all doomed, the sky is going to fall on my head."

His apocalyptic prediction that the end of the world was nigh was greeted with initial scepticism by Georgie Porgie Osborne (a much hated figure who had once made all the girls cry by cutting child benefit).

Old King Dole

Said Georgie Porgie, "Chicken Mervyn is behaving like a... well... like a headless chicken... except with a head. He is not helping Toyland with his doom-and-gloom.

"The truth is there has been a slight fall in acorns which has had a knock-on effect on Chicken Mervyn's head which has caused him to panic. There is nothing to worry about."

There was, however, an immediate run on the markets by a Little Piggy, though another Little Piggy did stay at home, which made the outlook more difficult to predict.

LATE NEWS: Sky Does Fall On Everyone's Head as World Ends Just as Chicken Mervyn Predicted

---

How *are* the markets this morning?

FTSE 100	5563.47	▲	17.83	**0.32%**
DAX	6099.81	▼	-33.37	**-0.54%**
CAC 40	3196.54	▲	1.07	**0.03%**
DOW JONES	12044.47	▲	208.43	**1.76%**
NASDAQ	2697.97	▲	57.99	**2.20%**
NIKKEI	5543.85	▲	19.45	**0.35%**
SHEPHERD'S BUSH	23p ◯	▼	-17.83	**-0.32%**

"This tabard's the best investment I ever made"

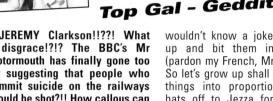
GLENDA SLAGG
Fleet Street's High Octane Four Star Top Gal – Geddit?

■ JEREMY Clarkson!!??! What a disgrace!?!? The BBC's Mr Motormouth has finally gone too far suggesting that people who commit suicide on the railways should be shot?!! How callous can you get!!? I'll tell you who should be put in front of a train and shot – the big-bellied bully boy of the BBC (That's the Boorish Broadcasting Corporation) – That's who?!!? And I'll volunteer to drive the train that shoots him!!?!

■ FOR crying out loud! What happened to the good old British sense of humour?!! Have we had our funny bones surgically removed? Jeremy Clarkson was making a JOKE!?! J-O-K-E?? (Geddit!!) Remember them?! The po-faced killjoys in the TUC wouldn't know a joke if it came up and bit them in the arse (pardon my French, Mr Editor!!?!). So let's grow up shall we and get things into proportion!!?!! And hats off to Jezza for reminding us amidst the doom and gloom that laughter is the best medicine!?

■ JEREMY CLARKSON!? Why do these journos play into his hands by giving him the oxygen of publicity!?!! He's trying to sell his DVD stoopid and you are just handing him free acres of advertising on a plate by telling him that you are sick of him or that you are taking your hat off to him!?!! Who cares?! Just put a sock in it!!!?

Byeee!!

 ## The Daily Courant
December 6, 1729

Calls For Celebrity In 'Joke' Furore To Be Sacked

A top celebrity cleric was forced to apologise last night for saying that poor Irish people should kill their children and sell them to the rich as meat.

"It was a bit of light-hearted banter," said Jonathan Swift, 58, Dean of St Patrick's Cathedral in Dublin. "I am sorry if it caused any offence to the publick."

This followed his "modest proposal" that "a young, healthy child, well nursed, is, at a year old, a most delicious, nourishing and wholesome food," which provoked more than 20,000 complaints.

"Dean Swift clearly needs a reminder of just whom he is talking about when he calls for infants to be eaten for dinner," said Dave Prentis, a prominent chorister from the Unison section. "Hanging's too good for him."

When told that the Dean was claiming that the whole thing was a joke, Mr Prentis said, "Well, it's a pretty poor one. Dean Swift is no Jeremy Clarkson, is he?"

That All-Purpose Strike Piece In Full

By Our Industrial Staff **Ed Bias**

YESTERDAY's day of action called by the trade union movement was a damp squib/ huge success as nearly 2 million people/hardly anyone at all took to the streets/went to work as usual.

Airports ground to a halt/ carried on as normal whilst most of the country's schools/a handful of the country's schools stayed open/stayed closed.

At major hospitals the story was the same/completely different. Hundreds of patients complained/paid tribute to the medical staff who left them to die on trolleys/ensured their life, saying operations were 100% successful.

The trade unions were absolutely delighted/bitterly disappointed by the high/ low turnout. One TUC leader boasted/confessed, "It's a slap in the face for the government/

Workers/Shirkers

ourselves, as nearly the entire country/two men and a dog registered their legitimate anger by withdrawing their labour/going shopping for Christmas presents in Westfield/ Bluewater/Lakeside."

Only the newspapers continued as normal by slavishly toeing the party line/making sure the party line was toed slavishly.

© All Newspapers.

A Taxi Driver writes

EVERY week a well-known cab driver is invited to comment on an issue of topical importance. This week **Mike Gove** (Cab No. 7742) on the TUC day of action.

Those strikes, eh guv? Holding the country to ransom. Makes you sick. They're just out for themselves. Kiddies missing school. Single mums forced to stay at home. Pensioners dying in hospitals. Bodies remaining unburied on the streets. Terrorists unable to get through immigration at Heathrow. The whole thing's a bloody mess, guvnor. There ought to be a law against it. I mean, in the old days, when I was on the NUS picket line, we were doing it for the public good. Not like this shower, selfish bastards, if you'll forgive my French. They should be strung up, if you ask me, it's the only language they understand because they don't teach Latin and Greek anymore. I 'ad that Arthur Scargill in the back of my cab once.

HERNEMAN

"Sorry, I can't remember a thing"

DAY 94 STARS TELL OF 'LIVING HELL' AT HANDS OF MEDIA

The inquiry heard evidence from a number of distinguished public figures, all of whom had suffered extreme distress after the serial invasion of their privacy

HM THE QUEEN

Her Majesty was close to tears as she told the inquiry of her years of harassment at the hands of the media. "My husband and I," she said, "have for many decades been hounded 24/7 by members of the press, causing untold unhappiness to ourselves, our children and, worst of all, our corgis.

"There are times," the monarch sobbed, "when Phil and I have seriously thought of jacking in the whole thing. Once, when they were long-lensing us over the Palace wall, he said, 'Sod this for a game of soldiers'. And even that appeared on the front page of the following Sunday's News of the World under the headline 'Philip's latest gaffe over defence cuts'."

MISS NANCY DELL'OLIO

Looking svelte and sexy, after posing for photographers outside the Law Courts, Miss Dell'Olio told Lord Leveson, "Your British press is a disgrace. Many days I am not even in the papers at all. My phone has never been hacked, even when I was with Sven. And then when I won Strictly Come Dancing they refused to print it, and told lies about me being voted out. Me, the sexiest, cleverest woman in the world. They have made my life a misery. Anyone less talented and brilliant than me would have killed themselves."

THE LATE SIR OSWALD MOSLEY

Looking as dapper and commanding as ever in his neat black shirt and highly polished jackboots, the former Fascist leader lashed out at "the lying vipers of the Jewish Bolshevik press". He told Lord Leveson, "They accused me of attending a Nazi rally where people made Fascist salutes and praised my friend Herr Hitler. It was a purely private occasion and the press had no right to intrude on my personal life. And now it is all anyone will remember about me – that I was some kind of a right-wing fanatic. I demand that the press should be strictly regulated, with harsh penalties for anyone who steps out of line, including death."

LORD LUCAN

Giving his evidence on a video link from "somewhere in Africa", and looking tanned and fit despite his 104 years, the Earl of Lucan told the inquiry how he had been forced to flee the country in 1974 as a result of a vindictive campaign of press harassment lasting several weeks. "The papers assumed that I had somehow killed our family's nanny and then felt free to indulge in an orgy of speculation about my private affairs. If it had not been for the support of close friends such as Jimmy Goldsmith and dear old Johnny Aspers, I might well have ended it all there and then by jumping off the ferry."

COMMANDER JAMES BOND R.N.

Giving evidence from behind a screen to protest his identity as a senior employee of the Secret Intelligence Service, Commander Bond told the judge that he had been repeatedly filmed in compromising situations with a long succession of attractive women. "These people will stop at nothing to exploit the public's taste for sexual titillation," he told Lord Leveson. "The fact that I choose to have fleeting affairs with these so-called 'Bond girls' in the course of my work is of no possible public interest, yet the media continually brands me as an irresponsible playboy with commitment issues. I am utterly sick of it. I have an important job, killing people and blowing up their secret headquarters, and sometimes when I see those cameras pointing at me, I'd like to blow them up too.

DAY 95 'MY EDITORS KNEW EXACTLY WHAT I WAS DOING,' FAMOUS JOURNALIST TELLS INQUIRY

MR LUNCHTIME O'BOOZE

The Fleet Street legend and "author of a thousand scoops", Lunchtime O'Booze, shocked the inquiry by producing a large scrapbook of cuttings which he said demonstrated the "depths to which I was forced to sink by my editors in order to get the big stories". He told the judge, "They are scum, worse than paedos, Your Honour, if you know what I mean. Andy Coulson and Rebekah Brooks are, in my book, as guilty as sin. They should both be strung up, because it is the only language they understand."

Mr O'Booze went on to tell the judge how the degrading practices into which he was forced by his editors had imposed on him such a strain that he had developed a drink problem.

"It was a living hell," he said. "I loved every minute of it."

Coming soon to the star-studded Leveson inquiry

- Jeffrey Archer
- Jonathan Aitken
- Jonathan King
- Ronnie Biggs
- Baroness Uddin
- Mrs Fred West

NEXT WEEK PANDAS CALLED TO GIVE EVIDENCE TO LEVESON

Tian Tian and Yang Guang will talk about press harassment and media intrusion into their private lives: "They kept writing about when we were going to have sex – to the point where we no longer wanted to do it, and our relationship broke down completely".

LEVESON INQUIRY
ALASTAIR CAMPBELL SPEAKS OUT!

The press print lies...

...and not just the ones I told them

NEVER TOO OLD

A new love story by Dame Sylvie Krin, author of *Heir of Sorrows* and *Duchess of Hearts*

THE STORY SO FAR: Octogenarian media tycoon Rupert Murdoch is being hounded by Lord Leveson who is raking up the painful past. Now read on...

AS darkness settled over Manhattan, a light burned in the penthouse suite of the iconic Skynewscraper Building overlooking New York's Central Park.

The world's most powerful mogul sipped his cup of cocoa as he sat morosely in his designer Hackett dressing gown and matching slippers.

On the 120" Shitachi plasma HD screen the proceedings of the official inquiry into press ethics in the UK were being beamed relentlessly across the globe.

Occasionally the elderly figure watching in the Parker Bowles armchair muttered the odd disapproving phrase: "Dingo's bum!"... "Swagman's dunny"... "Cobber's arse!!"...

But the dulcet tones of his ennobled nemesis on the television screen began to make him drowsy.

And who was that young woman who was now taking the stand? Her face seemed to be familiar, but he struggled to remember the name.

"Strewth!" he cursed to himself. "My memory's even worse than my son James', and I'm not even pretending!"

But now it was all coming back to him – that was Charlotte Church, the little cutie with the voice of an angel. How was it his flagship news organ had described her? *"Chavvy Charlotte in booze and fags sex shame".* So what the hell was she whingeing about now? Rupert suddenly felt tired and the years weighed heavily on his shoulders...

POP! went the cork as it exploded from the Jeropaxman bottle of KeepMumm's vintage champagne, to the delight of the assembled wedding guests who had been invited onto Rupert Murdoch's luxury yacht, the Belgrano 2.

And what a dazzling array of celebrities were there to witness his nuptials to his beautiful bride from the land of the beansprout, his very own Egg Fu Very Young, Wendi Deng.

There was British Prime Minister Tony Bliar, helpfully cleaning the tables and serving the canapés. And wasn't that TV's Ross Kamp having a playful domestic incident with his then partner, the flame-haired Rebekah Crooks? So many stars, so many names to remember...

"What would you like me to sing, Mr Murdoch?"

And there she was, the angel herself, the 13-year-old Charlotte Church, radiant in her traditional Welsh national costume, complete with bonnet, headscarf and leek.

But before he could answer, the bride herself appeared, looking stunning in her Yves Dropping St Laurent bridal gown and Karate black belt.

"You, girl!" she said, pointing at Charlotte. "You sing *Pie Jesu* for Lupert."

The innocent face of the voice of the valleys creased in a frown of confusion.

"But, Ms Deng," she said, "*Pie Jesu* is usually sung at funerals."

"You crever girl! You get idea straightaway! You go far," came back the immediate response from Rupert's Chinese fortune-hunter cookie. "Perfect song for old man like Lupert. Ha ha ha."

As the heavenly notes of Phwoaré's Requiem Mass soared high above the yacht and across the muddy stretch of Digger's Creek, Rupert thought to himself, *"Pie Jesu* wept! I'm not paying a bushwhacker's bean to this little trollope! I'll get the News of the Screws to turn her over..." Turn her over... Turn her over...

"**T**URN her over, Lupert! This very boring! We watch Shopping Channel now."

Rupert woke suddenly from his reverie to find his wife had returned and was now gazing fondly at advertisements for martial arts equipment.

He sighed. Outside a pale crescent moon was on the wane...

(To be continued)

The Eye's Controversial New Columnist

He gives it to you straight in the eye and all over your shoulder

This week I am very angry about these horrific stories told in the Leveson inquiry. Speaking as a famous and controversial columnist *(see photo)*, I know the lengths that some disreputable types can go to for their pound of flesh; I am always surrounded by vultures trying to get a photo of me. These vermin waggle things in my face! They call out to get my attention! They pretend to be my relatives! They even say disgusting things, like "Oo's a wuvwy wickle boy, den? Oo is? You is! You's a wubwy wickle chubby chops!" just to get a reaction from me, and if I so much as look in their direction, out come the cameras, and suddenly there are naked photos of me everywhere! Even on the television (next to the Sky box!) and I am left humiliated and unable to demand an apology from the so-called Press Complaints *(cont. p. 94)*

(cont. p. 94)

ME AND MY SPOON

THIS WEEK

RICKY GERVAIS

Do you have a favourite spoon?

Yes, it's the one I keep on the top shelf so that dwarves can't reach it. Tee hee hee!

Do spoons feature prominently in your work?

Yes, there's a very funny scene in my new series *Little Humour* where a dwarf and a mong have a fight over a spoon while Johnny Depp and Sting have a laugh!

That sounds offensive.

No, it's ironic, obviously, and you are too stupid to see it. In fact, you would have to be a mong to think that I'm being deliberately offensive to either mongs or dwarves. I'm laughing at people's reactions to mongs and dwarves, not mongs and dwarves themselves…you thick, short-arsed mong.

If we can get back to spoons for a minute…

Forget spoons. How about a column called *Me and My Spaz* – that would be funny and ironic, wouldn't it? Tee hee hee! You could ask mongs and dwarves if they've got a favourite spazzo! Which would highlight a taboo subject in a clever, post-modern and not-at-all-bullying way.

Has anything amusing ever happened to you in connection with a spoon?

Look, I'm laughing *with* spoons, not *at* them. I'm not spoonist. I'm trying to open up a debate about the nature of spoonism.

Thank you very much indeed.

Mong…dwarf…spaz…tee hee!

NEXT WEEK: *Stephen Merchant, "Me And My Merchant".*

POETRY CORNER

**In Memoriam
Norman St John Stevas
(1829-2012), aesthete and
former Minister for
the Arts**

So. Farewell
Then
Norman St John
Stevas.

You were best known
For your bitchy remarks
About Mrs Thatcher,
Whom you called
"The Leaderene".

But you were also famous
For your love of
Fine Art,
The Queen Mother,
The Pope and
Victorian bric-a-brac.

The obituaries called you
"Flamboyant", "theatrical",
"Fruity", "camp"
And "unmarried".
I think we get the idea.

E. St J. Thribb (117½)

**In Memoriam
Fabrice Muamba, Bolton
Footballer**

So. Farewell
Then
Fabrice
Muamba.

And welcome
Back.

Phew that
Was close.

They thought
It was
All over,
But happily
It isn't now.

Should
There be a
Minute's silence?

Or a minute's
Applause?

Funny old
Game,
Football.

E.J. Thribbulator (17½)

DIARY

TRIBUTES TO SIR JIMMY SAVILE

DAME A.S. BYATT

Curiously, I first became aware of Jimmy Savile when he appeared in those seminal television advertisements for the national railway system in the early to mid 1970s.

"This is the age" he would say, before adding, after the briefest of pauses, " – of the train". It was an extraordinarily powerful message. Prior to this, he would have alerted us to the essential paradox that – and here I quote from memory – "an away day is an offpeak ticket so it costs you less". It's meaning was both clear yet at the same time curiously opaque.

KARL LAGERFELD

I was mad for him! The blond hair, the tracksuits, the cigars. Mad for! Sir Jimmy was so sexy, hm? So gorgeous, so divine, like a beautiful pierrot in a painting by Watteau, hm?

Who cares for Dave Lee Travis? DLT is so COMMON, so DEMODE! No, Sir Jimmy is my muse! Did you ever see him on Dobov Zurbobs? His colourful tracksuits were so chic, so trendy, so SEXY! My Spring collection, it will be ALL Jimmy. My girls, they will be modelling my new eveningwear range in Jimmy wigs and Jimmy tracksuits walking down catwalk waggling their Jimmy cigars and saying "Arseabutt zat zen guysngals". And it will all be so powerful, so sexy, hm?

HRH THE PRINCE OF WALES

Sir Jimmy was one of those truly extraordinary characters who had no regard for what one might call one's social "position", whatever that might be, and always insisted on telling one the truth – no matter how painful! I'll never forget the day he took me "to one side" – I imagine he was dressed in one of those outlandish "psychedelic" suits of his! – and he looked me straight in the eyes and came out with it. "Now then, now then, boss – there's something I've got to tell you – urhurhuhrur – 'cos no one else will."

I took a deep breath and asked him to "give it to me straight", as it were.

"You're doing a great job, sir, and no mistake!"

It can't have been easy for him, but I'll always appreciate his quite extraordinary candour.

DR ROWAN WILLIAMS, ARCHBISHOP OF CANTERBURY

Jimmy was, in a very real way, a modern-day saint. So what does one mean by that intensely yet strangely numinous phrase "modern-day saint?" Clearly one is not referring to an elderly gentleman with a beard sitting on a cloud with a harp and a choir of angels! Far from it! I think we've got beyond that by now!! For one thing, Jimmy chose not to have a beard. That was entirely a matter for him, it is very much up to the individual. No, by "modern-day saint", I think one means something much more profound, something real yet at the same time intangible, something rather closer to "self-promoting disc jockey and television personality with irritating manner and limited vocabulary". Then again, he was so much more than that.

But what? It's a fascinating question, and I hope that, by raising it, one might do much to help kick-start a national debate.

V.S. NAIPAUL

Every week, he would promise "Jim'll Fix It".

He was bitterly mistaken. He never fixed anything of any importance. Despite the man's promises, the world remains a revolting, unworkable place. This means that his reputation is at an all-time low. He lacks credibility. He may have gained a knighthood, but he was never even considered for a Nobel Prize. "How's about that, then?" was the question he asked incessantly. The only answer was "dismal". He was a second-rater. Why should we be at all interested in this tedious fellow?

JOAN COLLINS

I was married to James for an all-too-brief few months in the 1930s, or was it the 1940s? We were young and carefree. Blackpool, Bournemouth, Skegness: we were seen everywhere together. In those days, one couldn't even take off one's bikini-top in public without being photographed, such was the remorseless appetite of the press! But then I bumped into the French President, Charles de Gaulle, when I was halfway-through changing my clothes on the beach at St Tropez. In his peaked snorkel and military trunks, Charles proved irresistible. The pair of us fell head-over-heels in love. Yes, I broke James's heart, and this time there was nothing he could do to fix it.

As told to CRAIG BROWN

DEUTSCHLAND ÜBER ELLAS

(surely alles? Ed.)

THE EYE'S MOST READ STORIES

Europe to Leave the EU

The leaders of France and Germany have urged calm after an announcement from Brussels that Europe was leaving the EU.

"It is clear now that the situation has reached the point where if Europe is to have any future it must be outside the EU," said a scared-looking foreigner.

"It is only by leaving Europe that Europe can prosper. From now on we'd like to be called Outer China."

Opera highlights

Mozart's
Don Berlusconi

THE DON is in high spirits after a lavish party in the Palazzo Fornicazzione attended by a large chorus of nubile courtesans and parliamentary advisers who perform the legendary Italian folk dance "La Bunga Bunga".

But his idyll is disrupted by the sinister figure of the Queen of the Right, Angela Merkel, who berates Silvio for his reckless life and tells him to mend his ways or face eternal damnation. The Don, however, laughs her to scorn, singing "Nessun Reforma".

But it is too late. An army of technocrats invade the palazzo singing "Billione e Tre" ("You Are €300 Billion in Debt") and drag Don Berlusconi into the fiery abyss.

The peasants rejoice in the downfall of Silvio and the elevation of his replacement Mario Monti, singing "Viva Monti Python" ("Always Look on the Bright Side of Life").

But their rejoicing is short-lived as a voice is heard from the depths: "Forza Italia!"

It is the Robber Baron himself vowing to return to life and wreak his revenge.

CAMERON'S MANSHION HOUSHE SHPEECH

I shay... why do people keep going on about the Bullingdon Club, what?

SIR FRED FIGHTS TO KEEP TITLE

I'm still Britain's Most Hated Man

FRED THE SHRED

'STRIP HIM OF HIS KNIGHTHOOD!'
National Clamour Grows

by Our Political Staff **India Knight**

HE's an embarrassment to the whole country! He's a disgrace to the nation!

He should never have been given a knighthood in the first place!

Yes, it's time to force Sir Bruce Forsyth to give back his ill-gotten gong and say, all together, "*Not* Knight to see you, to see you *not* Knight!" (*You're fired. Ed.*)

FRED GOODWIN
Those Revoked Titles In Full

- Lord Haw-Haw (*treason*)
- Lady Chatterley (*adultery*)
- Lady Gaga (*insanity*)
- The Dukes of Hazzard (*speeding*)
- Baron Samedi (*voodoo*)
- Baron Hardup (*theft*)
- Count Dracula (*assault*)
- Lady Godiva (*obscenity*)
- Lord Voldemort (*pure evil*)
- Lord of the Flies (*killing Piggy*)
- OBE Wan-Kenobi (*misuse of force*)
- CBE-3PO (*prissy*)
- Knight Rider (*talking to car*)
- The Earl-ly Learning Centre (*childishness*)
- Count Down (*using the word "wanker" before the watershed*)

The Daily Chain Mail
Friday, February 10, 1485

Lancelot Stripped of Knighthood Shock

by **Michael T.H. White**

BRITAIN'S top knight, Sir Lancelot Du Lac, has had his knighthood revoked over his behaviour during the collapse of Camelot.

Mr Lancelot, as we must now call him, had been the leading member of the very successful Round Table and had a dazzling career as "the most perfect knight in Christendom".

But his dalliance with a colleague's wife (Queen Guinevere, whom we cannot name for legal reasons) distracted him from his pursuit of the Holy Grail and brought about the disastrous collapse of the whole chivalric system in Britain.

A spokesman for Mr Lancelot

said, "No one saw the disaster coming, including top forecaster Merlin of Morgan Le Fay Grenfell Associates. It is unfair to lay all the blame on Lancelot – what do people expect him to do? Retire to a hermitage and then die from penitence and grief?"

ON OTHER PAGES
- **Should Bonking Sir Boris be in charge of London? p2** ● **Arthur to Give Back Bonus Sword p3** ● **Your Camelot Lucky Numbers Tonight p94**

 # Dave Snooty AND HIS PALS

BOO! DOWN WITH THE BANKERS! SHRED SIR FRED! BAN THE BONUS!

ER...DAVE, AREN'T THEY ALL YOUR FRIENDS?

YES - BANKER- BASHERS! JOLLY GOOD CHAPS!

ARE YOU TRYING TO **DISTANCE** YOURSELF FROM YOUR OLD CHUMS, DAVE...DAVE...DAVE?

SORRY - CAN'T HEAR YOU!

ISN'T THAT A U-TURN?

I'M SIMPLY URGING RESTRAINT, RESPONSIBILITY AND MODERATION...

...I.E. DON'T BE BEASTLY TO ME JUST BECAUSE I'VE DONE A U-TURN!

HE'S GOT NO BACK-BONUS EH READERS!?

...OR SHOULD THAT BE BANK-BONE?

FOR HE'S A **JELLY** GOOD FELLOW!

CITY

WHAT AN RBS-HOLE!

THAT'S UNFAIR -I'VE BEEN **CONSISTENT**. I'VE **CONSISTENTLY** DONE WHATEVER'S **POPULAR**!

THE Sun

Friday, February 10, 2012

IT'S ALL IN YOUR CURRANT BUNG!

TOP COPS IN DAWN SWOOP ON MYSELF

By Our Crime Correspondent **PHIL JAIL**

THERE were dramatic scenes in my office earlier today which I witnessed with my very own eyes.

A squad of burly policemen with search warrants forced their way into the News International building and led me away in handcuffs, charging me with "inappropriate payments to police officers".

In all my years as a crime correspondent I have never seen anything like it.

I asked Inspector Knacker, the officer commanding operation Stable Door, for a quote and he replied, "£250 in the old days, guv, but we're not allowed to do that anymore."

As I was then bundled into a Black Maria along with many of my colleagues including senior executives Ron Sleaze, Bill Pickup and Ivor Chequebook (but not James Murdoch because he knew nothing about it, honestly), I attempted to offer Inspector Knacker an agreeable lunch over which we could sort out the misunderstandings that had clearly arisen.

Inspector Knacker however, ignored my requests and issued me with a caution.

"I have to remind you, Phil," he said, "that anything you pay will be taken down the station and used to buy the lads a drink."

Nursery Times

·························· Friday, February 10, 2012 ··························

Tweedle Brothers

Dum In Veiled Attack On Dee

by Our Political Staff
Alice Throughthelookingglass-Thompson

Left to right: Dee and Dum

TWEEDLEDUM, the estranged brother of Tweedledee, who was once tipped to be the leader of the Mad Hattersley Tea Party, has returned to the political fray.

In what was seen as a coded criticism of his brother, Dum went up to Dee and hit him very hard on the head with a rattle.

Dum said, "You idiot! You are taking the party too far to the left and making us look anti-business".

"Contrariwise." replied Dee, "No wonder you're pro-business Fat Cat Boy, you're making a fortune and not paying any tax!"

He subtly then reinforced his point by whacking his brother back with his rattle.

Mr Alastair Dormouse then woke up from his sleep to say, "I think Dum is the man to lead us into Wonderland."

POLICE LOG

Neasden Police Station

0530 hrs 170 officers are to be redeployed for the foreseeable future onto Operation Hackbust. The target is to arrest the entire staff of the Sun newspaper for a range of criminal offences, including phone hacking, interception of private emails and attempting to bribe officers of the Neasden Police Force.

0600hrs Dawn raids carried out on 24 separate addresses of employees of News International, including the Sun's Quick Crossword editor, Sid Clue, the paper's Your Sun Weatherwatch reporter, Hugh Wotascorcher, and Page 3 girl, Tania Kitoff, the Ukrainian-born model who was last year voted "Neasden Station's Number One Topless Lovely".

0830 hrs The station's Custody Units are now over-full, necessitating the early release of a number of gang members being held on suspicion of minor offences, such as carrying offensive weapons, grievous bodily harm and multiple homicide. Miss Kitoff is still being questioned by a number of officers after refusing demands for "a strip search".

1030 hrs Following a call from Scotland Yard, 60 officers were deployed to provide round-the-clock surveillance on premises at 27 Livingstone Way, the home of Mr Al Qaeda, following his release earlier from HM Prison Long Lartin. Officers are instructed to escort Mr Al Qaeda to the Pricerite Road benefit office to collect entitlements due to himself and his family, ensuring that he is not subjected to harrassment from any members of the press not currently in custody.

1745 hrs Owing to operational pressures, Desk Sergeant Uxbridge was unable to respond to various messages left on the answering machine by members of the public, including a report for attendance at the Diane Abbott Shopping Mall, which was allegedly on fire and under siege from hundreds of young people in hoods and balaclavas.

1800 hrs Leaving party in The Star of Khomeini restaurant to say farewell to our former Chief Superintendent Ali Bulli who is sadly having to leave us again to serve another prison sentence. We all wish him well, but were able to comfort him with the knowledge that he will soon be joined by many of his former Neasden colleagues when they have been found guilty of taking bribes from the Sun journalists we arrested earlier.

Germans Accused Of Trampling On Greek Democracy

"I was only giving orders"

Those possible US responses to Iran in full

1. War

2. War

3. War

4. War

5. War

6. ~~Sanctions~~ *No*

7. Er...

8. ...That's War

"You know how we're all supposed to be in the same boat? We'd like to be in yours"

David Cameron An Apology

IN COMMON with all other Tory newspapers, we may in recent weeks have given the impression that back in December the prime minister had shown himself at the EU Summit in Brussels to be a brave and unswerving Eurosceptic who was not afraid to stand up to Europe and to boldly protect Britain's sovereignty at all costs. Headlines such as "Dave is the new Maggie", "Cameron is the new Churchill" and "PM is the new Henry V", may have misled readers into thinking that we somehow believed that by telling the EU that he was not prepared to go along with their treaty, Mr Cameron was in some way exercising a veto against yet another encroachment by the EU on Britain's powers of self-government. We now realise that there is not a jot or scintilla of truth in the above and that Mr Cameron is, in fact, a weak, cowardly, craven, gutless, unprincipled, treacherous, grovelling, cheese-eating surrender monkey who will stop at nothing to appease the Eurofanatics of Brussels who will not rest until they have removed every last vestige of Britain's power to govern herself. Today's headline, "EU to send in Gauleiter to run Britain as they did in Greece and Italy – Cameron runs up white flag", says it all. We apologise to our readers for any confusion to which our earlier reports may have given rise.

Foul-mouthed Character Not Based On Foul-mouthed Character

Alastair Campbell   Malcolm Tucker

SPIN doctor Alastair Campbell has revealed that his foul-mouthed, vitriolic character, made famous by the satirical Blair government, wasn't, as everyone assumed, based on the fictional, foul-mouthed, vitriolic Number 10 spin doctor Malcolm Tucker. He said, "No, I based my character on Miranda Hart's loveable character, 'Chummy', in BBC's *Call The Midwife*." *(Rotters)*

PLOTTERS GET SIX YEARS

By Our Crime Staff **Harry Plotter**

THE GROUP of extremists who gathered in a North London house to hatch a plan to blow up the Labour Party have been sentenced to six years in opposition.

A court heard that the ringleaders were fundamentalist Blairites who "preached hate" against Ed Miliband in order to justify their attempts to spread terror among backbenchers.

Ed Balls, 43, and Yvette Cooper, 42, claimed they were indoctrinated by a powerful spiritual "Imam" from the Middle East called Tony Blair, but their elaborate plot to take over the country was discovered by the counter-insurgency forces of the *Daily Mail*.

The Face of Evil

Critics were furious at what they called the leniency of the punishment.

Said one, who was too scared to give his name (Mr Ed M.), "Six years is not enough. They'll be back cooking up their evil lasagna before you can say, 'I'm going to lose the election'."

The Adventures of Mr Milibean

Fountain & Jamieson

'What is **Andrew Marr** really like?' Asks Her Majesty the Queen

Elizabeth Windsor has had unique access to the long-serving interviewer and here exclusively gives her inside view of the man they call "the Diamond Geezer"

WE ALL know the public face of Andrew, the dutiful broadcaster, the earnest journalist, the institutional figurehead of the BBC. But what of the Andrew behind the carefully constructed façade?

Whilst he accepts his responsibility of being constantly on television, Andrew is actually an intensely private man and those who know him well are largely bound by injunctions. *(Is this right? Ed.)*

But the real Andrew is charming, witty, incredibly well read and above all very keen to ingratiate himself with the Royal Family.

Andrew Ma'am

And let us not forget that Andrew has had regular audiences with all the Prime Ministers of the last 20 years. Said David Cameron, "Andrew surprises you with his acute questions and depth of knowledge. It is more like you are interviewing him!"

And he is no fool. Gordon Brown told me, "One minute he's all very jolly, the next he's asking you if you are a nutter and you're on medication."

Andrew Smarrm

It hasn't always been easy for Andrew – one thinks back to the *Annus Horribilis* when he was editor of the Independent – but he has triumphantly weathered the storms and emerged as the key national figure in Britain today without whom I cannot imagine having the will to carry on being Queen.

©Elizabeth R.

Special offer to Eye readers

THE *ANDREW MARR ROYAL ANNIVERSARY MUG*

ANDREW

60 Glorious Ears

GNOME Heritage is proud to offer a perfect lasting memento of the event of the millennium which can be treasured by you, your children, the children you thought were yours but turned out to be someone else's, and their children's children, or whatever.

This perfect mug is designed by top ceramicist Sir Peregrine Grayson (RA) and is hand-tooled from microwaveable Pissporcelain™ by the master potters of Hari in the Deathly Hallows region of North Korea.

Send now to
Marr Mug Offer,
Unit 94, The Asil Nadir
Industrial Estate, Dartmoor

60 glorious pounds *plus P&P*

BBC1 Lord Lucan Night

6.00pm Antiques Roadshow
The BBC is asked to appraise an old Lord Lucan conspiracy theory that's been gathering dust in the attic for nearly 40 years.

7.00pm Kill the Midwife
Britain's favourite midwife (Miranda Hart) is called out late one rainy night to an exclusive Belgravia address by Lady Lucan only to find Lord Lucan lying in wait with a candlestick to batter her to death in a heart-warming way.

8.00pm Top Gear Special
Jeremy Clarkson test drives a bloodstained Datsun to the coast. Will it get him all the way to Africa?

9.00pm Upstairs, Downstairs Basement
While Sir Hallum Holland and Lady Agnes entertain Lord Lucan and his family, the staff downstairs are having to deal with disposing of a suspicious body-sized package.

(That's enough Lord Lucan, Ed.)

Lookalikes

Befuddled old man **Mr Magoo**

Sir,
Since Monday 13 February 2012, The Independent has been printing photographs of an 80-year-old befuddled old man who does not seem to know what is happening and who just happens to be chairman of NI, in place of photographs of Mr Magoo. Someone ought to be held accountable for this mistake!

WALDO (Greg Vanetzian),

Via email.

Hancock **Strauss-Kahn**

Sir,
Are they related?

PAUL BRIDGE,

Via email.

Dissident **Director**

Sir,
It appears that theatre director Sir Peter Hall and Chinese dissident Ai Weiwei are long-lost twin brothers.

ALAN BUNTING,

Harpenden, Herts.

Droopy **Cartoon character**

Sir,
I can't help noticing the striking similarity between the footballing manager Harry Redknapp, and the reknowned cartoon character Droopy. I am convinced they are related.

ROBERT WARD,

Via email.

Martian **Cheryl**

Sir,
The recent pictures of Cheryl Cole sporting her elegant new bouffant at the Olivier National Theatre reminded me of the Martians in the hit film Mars Attacks. They must surely be related.

Sincerely,
DANIEL JEORY,

Via email.

Liam the Fox **Robert the Bruce**

Sir,
First Liam Fox turns up on his friend's business card, now here he is on a Scottish banknote (sporting state-of-the-art MoD combats). He bears a striking resemblance to warrior king Robert the Bruce, and is in the same line of work – surely they must be (distantly) related?

Yours,
BRECK MACGREGOR,

Via email.

Pane in glass **Pain in...**

Sir,
When looking through the photographs I took on a recent visit to Sudeley Castle in Gloucestershire, I was struck by the resemblance between this image in a stained glass window and the Member for Corby and East Northamptonshire, Louise Mensch.

Kind regards,
RACHEL CARSON,

Via email.

Freddie **Vince**

Sir,
I knew I had seen that hat somewhere before. Vince Cable and Mr Krueger, related?

PHIL HANKIN,

Via email.

Hunt **Giggs**

Sir,
Did any of your readers notice the resemblance between Ryan Giggs and Jeremy Hunt? Both appear to be connected through current affairs and texting. I have never seen them in the same room.

BOB JONES,
Stone, Staffordshire.

New Queen **Old Queen**

Sir,
Considering the striking similarity between Boy George and the Duchess of Cambridge, could it be that Boy George has been misunderstood for many years?

A. TOWNSHEND,

Via email.

Conductor **QC**

Sir,
As an avid fan of both The Leveson Inquiry and On The Buses, I couldn't help noticing the remarkable similarities between QC for News International, Rhodri Davies, and On the Buses' cheeky chappy Jack Harper (played by Bob Grant). Mayhaps Mr Davies would care to appear in a revival of the show?

JAMIE MEAKES,

London.

Mark **Caligula**

Sir,
Has anybody noticed the increasing similarities (physical and rhetorical) between John Hurt's depiction of Caligula in the BBC's "I Claudius" and Mark Zuckerberg of Facebook?

WILLIAM LOWNDES,

Hong Kong.

Inquisitor

Misfit

Sir;

Has anyone else noted the uncanny resemblance between Santa Claus's misfit son Arthur Christmas, star of the eponymous animated film, and Jeremy Paxman, of Newsnight and University Challenge fame? It can be no coincidence that the sneering inquisitor is never seen on our tv on Christmas Eve!

STEVE HOPKINS,

Via email.

Peter Hill

Ribena berry

Sir;

I've been watching the Leveson inquiry with great interest and wondered if any other readers noticed the striking likeness between the small, purple, spherical thing on the screen being squeezed for its juices and a Ribena berry? Are they by any chance related?

Yours &c.,
ALASTAIR BRENT,

Via email.

Jimmy

Johann

Sir;

I wonder if your readers have noticed the striking resemblance between Labour's new leader in Scotland, Johann Lamont, and pantomime superstar Wee Jimmy Krankie?

I don't suppose, considering the Krankies' track record...!?!

DAVID HAY,
Glasgow.

Mitt Romney

Augustus Maywho

Sir;

While my two young children were enjoying coverage of the US primaries they couldn't help but notice that the Republican candidate Mitt Romney bears an uncanny resemblance to the Mayor of Whoville.

Yours,
ANDREW STOKES,

Via email.

Rihanna

Miss Piggy

Sir;

I wonder if, perchance, any of your readers have noticed the startling resemblance between Miss Piggy and Rihanna?

PHILIP BLUNT,

Via email.

Comic

Comic

Sir;

Having recently "got into another fine mess" with this funny little man, I was struck by how similar he was to great comic Stan Laurel. I wonder if they might be related?

Yours,
TONY CHAPMAN,
Cambridge.

Physicist

Physicist

Sir;

It can't have escaped your attention that Professor Peter Higgs (of boson fame) is none other than Isaac Newton! I'm sure I've seen them in the same place at the same time (although I can't be completely certain about that...).

W. HEISENBERG,

Via email.

Barry

Christine

Sir;

Did any of your readers notice the striking resemblance between the eternally youthful songster Barry Manilow and Christine Lagarde, leader of the International Monetary Fund, who told us in no uncertain terms last week that we in Britain have absolutely nothing to sing about for the foreseeable future?

Yours dispiritedly,
LOLA (EX-SHOWGIRL),

Via email.

Old reprobate

Indomitable Duke

Sir;

On a recent trip to the superb Leonardo exhibition I observed an acclaimed da Vinci sketch depicting a group of cheery old reprobates, one of whom bears an uncanny resemblance to our own indomitable Duke of Edinburgh. Closer examination showed this picture is owned by none other than Her Majesty the Queen. Methinks these two men must be related, but let's keep it from the old fugger, Mohamed Al-Fayed.

Yours,
L. BOOTH,

Via email.

Barking

Barking

Sir;

The similarity between a sad-looking bitch and a former Murdoch executive is too great to be mere coincidence.

Yours,
TED FORREST,

Sheffield.

Dobby

Dougy

Sir;

Has anybody noticed the similarities between Dobby, house elf, and Douglas Alexander, MP?

PIPPA WALLIS,

Via email.

Dave

d'Eon

Sir;

The similarity between Chevalier d'Eon, the famous 18th century transvestite and Rt Hon David Cameron PM, is uncanny. Are they by any chance related?

MIDEASTDREW,

Via email.

What you will see...

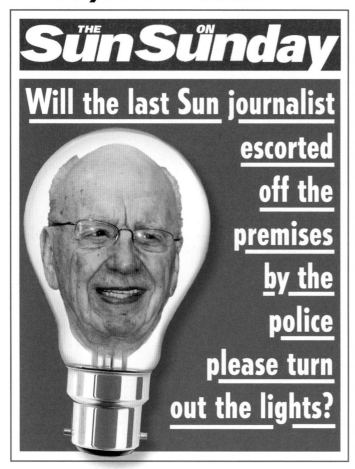

THE Sun on Sunday

Will the last Sun journalist escorted off the premises by the police please turn out the lights?

● **Mystic Meg** fails to predict that she is going to jail like everyone else

● **Rod Liddle** – 'Bang me up! It's the only language I understand'

● **Jeremy Clarkson** test drives the new Black Maria

PLUS SUNDAY NEWS IN LEGAL BRIEFS

● WPC Sabrina Anderson, 19, from Wigan is very excited that the Sun is getting published on a Sunday!

Sabrina says, "Forget the KNOCKERS, Rupert! Everyone with short MAMMARIES will forget about the News Of The World and flock to The Sun on Sunday!

"And just think of all those extra yummy Sun on Sunday journos I can BANG up! And even better, they'll give me a WAPPING PACKET for giving them a TIT-OFF about when they're going to get BUSTED!"

AND HAGAR THE HORRIBLE

There's more fun in the slammer!

Omnipotent Being's Amazing Act of Creation

There was widespread celestial joy last night as the supreme deity Rupert Murdoch created a new Sun within seven days.

Said a Murdoch spokesman, bearded disciple Trevor Kavanagh, "On the sixth day Rupert created the Sun on Sunday and He saw that it was rubbish."

He added, "It only goes to show that Rupert is a supreme being – superior to God in every way. God was stupid enough to sacrifice his only son. You won't catch Rupert doing that."

THE Sun on Sunday

Sunday, February 26, 2012

The Sun of God

A new column by the Archbishop of York, Dr J.C. SENTAMU

Today I am singing that great old hymn 'Jesus wants me for a Sun-reader'!

WHAT a fantastic honour for a humble little Archbishop like me to be invited by none other than the great Rupert Murdoch to pen a weekly column in his brilliant new Sunday newspaper!

Because, you know, God is the god of forgiveness. It doesn't matter what terrible things you've done, it's never too late to start again and to be given a second chance.

For instance, let's imagine that you are the proprietor of a newspaper that has brought shame on you by committing every kind of sin.

You are condemned by everyone. It seems that you can never be forgiven.

But that's where God comes in. Because for him it's never too late.

Just when you thought your world had come to an end, a miracle occurs!

As the Bible tells us, God worked very hard for six days and on the seventh day he put his feet up and relaxed with a copy of the new Soaraway Sun on Sunday.

They talk about rejoicing in heaven when a sinner repents.

All I can say is that there's certainly a really big party going on up there today, to celebrate the resurrection of the old News of the World in its shining new guise as the Risen Sun!

It's like Easter and Christmas both come at once!

© *The Good News of the World Bible Society, in co-operation with the SPNC (the Society for the Promotion of News Corp.)*

"We've trained him to remember our pin number"

Whole world to lose AAA rating

By Our Economics Staff **Hugh Knows**

THE world's financial markets were plunged into chaos last night when the ratings agency Badmoody and Pisspoore downgraded all the countries of the world from AAA to ZZZ, after finding that the global outlook had changed from "reasonably stable" to "utterly catastrophic".

The agency's lead analyst, Ms Jane Calamity, explained the thinking behind the new international ratings.

"We suddenly noticed yesterday," she said, "that Greece hasn't got a chance of paying back the hundreds of billions of euros everyone is lending them, so not only are they going bust but so is everybody who has lent them money, even more so when

Greece is followed by all the other countries they've lent money to, including Portugal, Ireland, Italy and Spain.

"Then, we reckon, when these countries default this will have a domino effect right across the eurozone, which will not only mean that Germany and France are bust, but also all those countries outside the euro area, including Britain, America, China and every other country you've ever heard of."

Ms Calamity concluded, "Perhaps the most worrying thing of all is that when every nation on earth has run out of money there will be no one left to pay for our ridiculous ratings system, which is why we have had to downgrade our own ranking to z-z-z-z-z".

"And you say you never saw any of the signs?"

HOW PUTIN WON ELECTION

I trust I can count on your support?

PRIVATE EYE opens its doors and opens your wallets *(surely "minds"? Ed.)* in a fun-packed festival, with hundreds of talks, lectures, debates, workshops and tickets still available – eye.co.uk/desperateforcash, #pleasecome.

Visitors will get to see the Eye's top contributors in action and be able to engage in producing the magazine as it happens. Key interactive events include:

➡ **Help Glenda Slagg write her hard-hitting current affairs column. You decide if she just loves Ken Barlow or, alternatively, if she is sick to death of him. Or both.**

➡ Join Lunchtime O'Booze in the pub as he continues his forensic investigation into the state of Britain's pubs.

➡ **Look after Polly Filler's toddler, Charlie, for the weekend, as her hopeless au pair from Syria, Assada, has gone home and her useless partner, Simon, is too busy watching the Eye's live open interview with top music act, Jason Mumsnet...**

➡ Go on a demo with Dave Spart – on Sunday he will be marching on behalf of the Hampstead Socialist Collective Alliance-Against-Charging-For-Swimming-In-The-Ponds-And-The-War-In-Afghanistan.

➡ **Open the door for Dame Sylvie Krin as she steps out of her Rolls-Royce (DSK1) and delivers her latest instalment of "Never Too Old..."**

➡ Contribute to the Eye's exciting Messageboards by calling other contributors "wankers" and comparing their views to Hitler...
And much, much more!

Join the Eye on its exciting journey from being a newspaper to being an online events company. (Is this right? Ed.)

HUGE MEDIA CORPORATION ACCESSES PRIVATE COMMUNICATIONS

by Our New Technology Staff **Konnie Haq**

ONE of the most powerful media organisations in the world has admitted deliberately targeting personal emails for commercial gain.

Google, for it is they, have confessed to monitoring millions of their users, and then exploiting

the sensitive information by then selling it to advertisers and having a laugh at which websites you have been visiting.

Said Rupert Murdoch, "This is an incredible intrusion into personal privacy on an industrial scale. I wish I had thought of it."

'BRITAIN NOW THE MAJOR THREAT TO WORLD PEACE'

by Our South Atlantic Staff **Adele Penguin**

IN AN astonishing 5-hour tirade to the United Nations, Argentina's foreign minister Señor Jingo claimed that David Cameron is the biggest threat to world peace since Adolf Hitler (now living quietly in a suburb of Buenos Aires).

"First," said Señor Jingo, "Britain committed an act of unprovoked military aggression against my country after we had peacefully invaded the Malvinas under my patriotic and democratically unelected predecessor General Fascistieri.

"Then, 30 years later, they send their entire navy, the nuclear-armed HMS Dinghy, to impose a reign of terror across the whole of the South Atlantic.

"Finally," said Argentina's top diplomat, "these colonialist British warmongers commit the most provocative breach of world peace of all by deliberately sending to the Malvinas the Queen's grandson, Prince William, as a member of Queen Elizabeth's most feared elite special forces combat unit, the RAF's Search and Rescue Sheep Which Have Fallen Over A Cliff Service."

Sr Jingo called on the UN to send an international task force to save the Malvinas from "this unparalleled act of genocide that makes Syria look like one of those famous British picnics that we have seen on repeats of Downton Abbey".

Sr Jingo's speech was hailed last night by the legendary Hollywood actor Sean Penn as "the finest example of political oratory since Kate Winslet's acceptance speech at the 2009 Oscars".

'I NOW BELIEVE IN GLOBAL WARMING' reveals Lord Lawson

I am the happiest man in the world! At the age of 97, not only have I found a new exciting blonde partner half my age, it also turns out she is incredibly rich.

All of which has led me to revise my well-known position on climate change. I can now tell you that around Chateau Lawson, my little place in south-west France, the temperatures have recently been rising to record levels!

Phew, what a scorcher, as we say in Bordeaux. The way things are going, I confidently expect the ice caps to be

Hot or what?

melting and sea levels to rise by 100 feet any minute now!

© *The Global Phwoarming Policy Foundation*

"...carefully fold the egg whites into the mixture – done... For fuck's sake, woman, you've bolloxed the whole fucking thing up, you stupid fucking useless cow..."

Nursery Times

·············· Friday, 24 February, 2012 ··············

TAX BREAK FOR MARY POPPINS

by Our Economics Staff **Nanny State McFee**

Middle-class families were delighted yesterday when the Government promised financial incentives for home helps to assist working mothers.

Said one parent, Mrs Banks, "This is very good news. It means we can employ Mary Poppins to take the children on jolly holidays and educational trips to meet chimney sweeps, allowing me to devote my time to campaigning for votes for women."

Her husband, bank worker Mr Banks, said, "The financial incentive is excellent, amounting to tuppence – which means that I can either invest prudently, fruitfully and frugally in railways to Africa or dams across the Nile, or alternatively I could buy a bag of bird seed from an old lady sitting on the steps of St Paul's Cathedral".

Most delighted of all was child carer Ms Poppins who had recently flown in on a cloud from London. She described the scheme as, "Supercalifragilisticexpiali-davidcameron!"

On Other Pages

● *Old Mother Hubbard told to sell dog and get a job* **p. 2**

● *Fiddlers Three lined up for Old King Cole's Jubilee concert* **p. 3**

● *Should Ali Baba be sent home on the first magic carpet?* **p. 94**

Those Greek Tragedies in Full

Sophocles

Oedipus Rex The Economy

Ancient Greece is in ruins thanks to the blind actions of a hopeless Greek motherf****r. (PG)

Aristophanes

The Frogs

The French join the Greeks' heroic fight against German domination.

Europides

We Want Our Money Bacchae

(This is terrible. You're fired. Ed.)

DIARY

JONATHAN MEADES' A-Z OF CHILDREN'S TELEVISION

ANDY Pandy: The incremental yet covertly unsustainable susceptibility of Andrew Pandy to the obtrusive valedictory remark is overtly exemplified in his obstinately tiresome refrain, "Time to go home, Time to go home, Andy is waving goodbye". Yet on the day immediately following the preceding day he inevitably reappears, ready to weary us again with his quasi-fascistical salutes, the only excuse for which is his role as an examplar of incompetent puppetry, the indisputably shoddy mechanisms of his strings made visible by the overwattaged glare.

BEAR, Paddington: The sight of this Peruvian dwarf inexpertly masquerading as a nondescript caniform bearing a suitcase or valise neither betokens credibility nor denies credulity.

CAT, Top: Feline delinquent biped, sparsely whiskered and boastfully inarticulate yet insistently demanding.

DAWG, Deputy: Slovenly law-enforcer who never rises beyond his avowedly secondary ranking despite relentlessly wholehearted courting of sordid popularity: his near-nudity and resentful gawkiness represent the death gurgle of a civilisation.

DIBBLE, Officer: Uniformed sub-McCarthyite disciplinarian, inexpert, obese, ill-educated.

DOO, Scooby: Execrably drawn canine mouthpiece for the universally preached, seldom practised, utterly trite and entirely unrealistic doctrine of infantilistic spiritualism.

DO, Yabba Dabba: Quasi-Dadaist outcry of antediluvian cross-dresser Fred Flintstone.

DOUGAL: Hirsute monosyllabic draught-excluder from Magic Roundabout (Le Manege Enchante).

DUMPTY, Humpty: Triumphalist ovoid wall-dweller tellingly transmogrified into offbeat omelette.

ERMINTRUDE: The history of Ermintrude, the doggedly unrealistic vache on Le Manege Enchante (see DOUGAL), Serge Danot's peculiarly obtuse and quasi-imbecilic experiment in sub-utopian neo-fascism, also represents a parallel history of bovicularine languorosity.

FLOWER Pot Men: It is emblematic of the deep conservatism of the British countryside that these two feeble artisans, aka William and Benjamin, should opt to remain domiciled a deux in a terracotta receptacle du jardin.

GRANGE Hill: The point about Grange Hill is that the education it provides, if education it can be said to be, is not conditional on authoritarianism; rather, it is the product of an essentially Rousseauesque belief in the primacy of the untutored.

HONG Kong Phooey: My ignorance of this nevertheless paltry aberration of a canine detective remains conditional on my refusal to manipulate the knobular control on my television towards the requisite channel.

IVOR the Engine: Characteristically massive in scale, self-consciously futuristic in form, decidedly rediffusionite in outlook, and determinedly unfit for travel, Ivor the Engine remains an unashamed misnomer, having been constructed wholly from cardboard.

JACKANORY: Tiresomely trite narratives unsuited to all but the most ignorant viewers.

JASON: An ostentatiously argonautical name forced upon the first Blue Peter cat by the Fuhrer Noakes.

JERRY, Tom and: Anti-authoritarian rodentalist propaganda.

KNOCKOUT, It's a: It is undeniable that to dress as an unrealistic courgette and leap-frog over cushions is to transport oneself a Dante-esque world beyond redemption.

LOO, Looby: Unfeasible quasi-rural female who resides in le panier picque-nicque with two male co-basketeers, Andrew Pandy and Teddy.

MAGPIE: One for a cause or occasion for grief or regret, two for a mental state of happiness or well-being, three for a pre-adolescent female homo sapiens: the theme tune of this bi-weekly series was, like VD or TB, considered catchy.

MUTLEY: Few races were less wacky, more tediously circular nor more unforgivably inconclusive than those in which Mutley and Dick Dastardly were forced to compete.

NOAKES, John: "Down Shep!" Risibly demanding, boorishly monosyllabic and quasi-fascistic, this was the inane yell of society's Little Man, that most disreputable and meglomaniacal of nature's nondescripts.

NOG, Noggin the: Pontificating arch-bore of indeterminate parentage.

OKE: Popular ignorance of the way in which Diane Louise Jordan's Summer expedition to Japan in 1991, which resulted in the naming of the Blue Peter cat "Oke", is of such magnitude that one can only suppose that state education remains a duo-terminological contradiction.

PITSTOP, Penelope: Pitstop's sluttishness, combined with her psychopathic, Clarksonian lust for speed demands comparison with the more refined and coquettish appeal of her namesake Lady Penelope, who, with her neo-Lawrentian chauffeur Parker, remains unchallenged in her primacy.

PLAY School: It is one of the great fallacies of 21st century civilisation that these two antonyms should be forcibly adjuncted. "Here's a house, here's a door. Windows, 1,2,3,4." Four windows for an entire house is indicative of architectural neglect.

PURVES, Peter: The biological and intellectual superior of Noakes, Purves exercised the minoritarian will towards programmatic dominance, but can be seen to have succeeded only in the relatively abstruse area of overnight intercourse with Singleton.

QUICK Draw McGraw: Anthropomorphism reached its upper level of experiential absurdity in the quotidian notion that a horse not only wears a hat and kerchief but also enforces law in the Wild West by effortlessly brandishing a loaded pistol in each frontal-based hoof.

RUBBLE, Barney: Flintstone's deuteragonist lickspittle.

SMURFS: De Smurfen parade their truncated Netherlandishness in a vivid mortuary blue.

TANK Engine, Thomas the: The popular obeisance of the rampant dehumanising of industrial transport is encapsulated in Thomas, whose wide-eyed pusillanimity prompts anything from vague resignation to muted indifference.

WEED, Little: Her place in the flowerpot is unconditional on her silence.

YOGI Bear: Sub-normal counter-jumping sidekick of the resolutely bourgeois Boo Boo.

ZEBEDEE: Spring-posteriorated, unforgivably moustachioed, gaudily repetitive, the malodorous Zebedee remained, predictably, an enthusiastic collaborator in Vichy France.

As told to CRAIG BROWN

BRITAIN OUTLINES AFGHAN EXIT STRATEGY

❶ Goodbye   ❷ Good luck

HOW IT WILL WORK

1 Phased withdrawal of troops from British Army by enforced redundancies

2 Build up of troops in Job Centre

3 Deployment of troops in stocktaking duties in Tesco (unpaid) as part of Operation Shelf Stack

4 Afghanistan now clear of British troops ready for Taliban-style democracy to take over and *(That's enough. Ed.)*

"Careful, lads, the Afghan army's covering our backs"

Eating and Drinking Can Kill, Says Government

*by Our Health Staff **Wilfred D'Eath***

A NEW official study has shown a startling correlation between the consumption of all forms of food and drink and the incidence of fatality in the population of the UK as a whole.

The study's remarkable finding is that almost all of the people who died in Britain last year did so after consuming food, drink or both.

A staggering 100 percent of all those who died of heart attacks had, in the period leading up to their death, eaten or drunk at least one unit of a foodstuff or beverage.

And the figures are even worse when it comes to all forms of cancer, where the alarming link between consumption and eventual death is at its most marked.

Said the Chief Medical Officer last night, "We are hoping to make a start on tackling this national crisis by putting health warnings on all food and drink products and making it illegal to eat or drink inside public buildings such as pubs, restaurants and cafes.

"If people wish to kill themselves, they will have to do so either in the privacy of their own home (but not their car) or outside in the street, in groups of fewer than 10 persons, at least six metres from a doorway."

'1000 WOMEN HAVE SLEPT WITH ME,' claims TV's Ken Barlow

by Our Media Staff **Corrie Corfield**

The star of Coronation Street, Bill Roache, has made a sensational revelation whilst being interviewed on ITV by Piers Moron.

"I just start talking," admitted Roache, "and women just fall asleep. In huge numbers."

When I asked Roache to confirm this, he told me, "It never fails. It's almost as if I am terrifically boring."

He then said something else, but unfortunately I felt very drowsy and z-z-z-z-z

Late News

● Figure rises to 1001.

THE TIMES

TV Highlights

Sharia Law

Channel 5 11pm

Less popular follow-up to LA Law. This week, maverick Saudi cop Mohammed Sharia is given 24 hours to stop a woman driving a car.

LIVINGSTONE TAX SHOCK

The polls say 50% of Londoners support me...

...but I hope to get that rate down to 20% by the time the election's over

---

Letters to the Editor

The Big Drought

Sir, Today I saw the first vulture of spring. Sitting in my study looking out at the arid savannah of Tunbridge Wells, I could not help but notice the charming bird of prey alighting on the carcass of a dead wildebeest as it rotted in a cloud of flies.

Does this mean that winter is finally over and we here in Kent can at last look forward to the delightful sight of the early cacti flowering in the dried up watering holes of the dustbowl of England?

MAJOR WALTER SHORTAGE
The Old Pumping Station,
Tunbridge No-Wells.

The Adventures of Mr Milibean

Fountain & Jamieson

Pseudo Names Pseudo Names

...With so much doom and gloom around we have all decided to take off, leaving on the next jet plane. Don't know when we'll be back again.

OMAH BAGS
R. PACT
ANNA REDD
D. TEGO.

...It is with some relief that I can finally put pen to paper now the acute pain in my arm has gone.

DENNIS L. BEAU.

...Do you think any toffs would contribute to Pseudo Names if you asked them? Seems pretty improbable to me.

HAYLEY N. LAKELY.

...I just wanted to thank Greece for all the uncertainty its financial situation has caused.

F. HARRY STOWE.

...The article in Eye 1300's Funny Old World about the coffee enema brought back some painful memories.

R. STORNOWAY.

...As one of your (no doubt legion) admirers here in Spain, I've intended to write to your esteemed organ on many occasions over the years. Unfortunately, though, before I get pen to paper I always seem to forget the point I wanted to make.

SEÑOR MOMENT.

...To cap a bothersome year, Miriam and I look unlikely to be invited to Heather Mills' again next Christmas. This year's festive prank went down VERY badly.

NICK CLEGG.

...I think I know what this year will mean to most of us.

MAUREEN DEBT.

...As a budding young industrialist I am incensed that President Sarkozy claims that we British have "no industry left"!

ZAC RAY BLURR.

...Here in Greece, many of us welcome the long-overdue return of firm government.

MILLIE TREE-HUNTER.

...I've often thought it would be nice to see in your pages a feature on classic films of yesteryear. But then again, I'm not particularly bothered.

FRANK LIMIDERE.

...Does anyone know just why Job Centre staff are laughing at me?

HUGH BEE (40).

...What will vulnerable people do after Lansley's Health Bill is passed?

DIANNE SUFFER.

...As a proud member of the working class who has risen to a high-ranking position in H.M. Prison Service I am getting rather fed up with the tiresome caricatures constantly trotted out each fortnight in your 'Yobettes' cartoon.

GORE BLIGHMEY (GOVERNOR).

...Is it O.K. to eat roast lamb on Easter Sunday?

AGNES DAY.

...Honestly, resorting to foodstuffs pronounced in a Birmingham accent (Roy Skrispies, Eye 1308) is a sure sign that this childish nonsense has gone too far.

CHIPSON GROIVY

...If your recent spate of letters from people with made up names sounding like foodstuffs spoken in a Brummie accent goes on much longer, you'll still be printing them when Christmas rolls around.

MIN SPOYS.

...Foodstuffs in a Brummie accent? As the star of an advertising campaign for a brand of peanuts, Noddie Holder might find something to celebrate in that.

CARMEN FIELDER-NOYCE,
CARL ZAGREB,
D. BOYCE,
VIGO WYLDE.

...Can the Diamond Jubilee street party food equal that served in Smethwick (near Birmingham) in 1953 [sic]?

GILLIAN TROYFUL.

...I would like to take this opportunity to assure your readers that no tools are left in my vehicle overnight.

M. TEEVAN.

...So incensed am I by the government's plans to limit tax relief on charitable donations that I am, at this very moment, drowning my sorrows.

PHIL N. THROE (pissed).

...Watching Boris, Ken and the other two hopeful Mayoral candidates debating recently, I was struck by the sincerity of their pledges to do more and cost us less.

M.T. PROM (Mrs).

...Why have I lately been getting the overwhelming feeling that everyone is trying to wind me up?

RAINE JERS.

...Let's not make a drachma out of a crisis.

U. ROE
DES ASTOR.

...The pathetic "Raine Jers" in the latest issue is the final straw. My letters are much funnier and consistently overlooked. Is it cos I am black?

RACHELLE D'SCRIMINATION.

...The postal service here in rural France can be shockingly slow sometimes, but I do hope this reaches you in time for your 50th anniversary edition.

HENRI TARD.

...Many readers will empathise with Monsieur Henri Tard (Eye 1315) and his delays with correspondence from France. I can remember when I was a young girl England had an excellent mail service that was both fast and inexpensive.

PENNY POST.

...I could tell Lord Leveson a hundred incredible stories.

D. CAMERON.

...Due to the continued barrage of stories attacking local government, we feel that we can no longer receive your publication.

COUNCILLOR SUBSCRIPTION.

...Mr Boyle's Olympic Opening Ceremony seemed a little higgledy piggledy.

WILLY NILLY.

...We are all a bit fed up with being deployed at the last minute to fill in for G4S at the Olympics, it's been a tough year what with Afghanistan, etc. Still, no point in moaning.

SOLDIER RON.

...We're absolutely sick of the Olympics and can't wait for it to be all over.

CHLOE SINGH
SARAH MOANY.

...I've read this column for ages, but I still don't really understand it.

WASAD AL ABAHT.

Art Attack

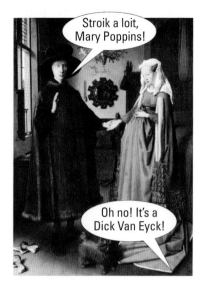

Stroik a loit, Mary Poppins!

Oh no! It's a Dick Van Eyck!

"Not **the** Napoleon Bonaparte?"

I was framed

(& Caravaggio)

"WRITE NOVEL – COMPOSE LIGHT OPERA – PAINT PORTRAIT – This looks like a job for Renaissance Man!"

SPECIAL RELATIONSHIP SPECIAL
PHOTO BROMANCE

We just clicked...

...as have all the cameras!

Say "cheesy"!

It was love at first flight

Pass the sick-bag!

It's a gay marriage of convenience

THE HISTORY OF THE SPECIAL RELATIONSHIP

Margaret Thatcher and Ronald Reagan

George Bush and Tony Blair

Gordon Brown and the man who looks after the toilet

OBAMA'S SPEECH IN FULL

Stroik a light, Mary Poppins... blimey... I'm chuffed to bits... apples and pears... let's have a good old natter on the dog and bone... chim chiminey... jellied eels and no mistake.... rub a dub dub.... top notch don'tcha know.... meet the trouble and strife... bubble and squeak... knees up Mother Brown... supercalifragilisticexpialido-cious... Afghanistan... oh no, I've ruined it and it was going so well.

© The Dick Van Dyke Institute For International Relations 2012.

PRINCE HARRY DISGRACES ROYAL FAMILY SHOCK

by Our Royal Staff **Prince Andrew Marr**

AT THE end of his royal tour of South America and the West Indies, commentators expressed their dismay at Prince Harry's conduct whilst representing Her Majesty the Queen.

"This is not what we expect from senior members of the Royal Family," said one observer.

"Everywhere he went he behaved himself and went out of his way not to offend anyone.

"It was frankly not embarrassing," he continued. "Where were the jokes about watermelons? Why didn't he play golf with a dictator and accept a freebie into the bargain? He didn't even get drunk, smoke dope or wear a Nazi uniform."

Ginger Nuts

His grandfather is said to be "dismayed" at the younger generation's lack of antics whilst on official duties.

Said one source close to HRH the Duke of Edinburgh, "What the

hell is the blithering idiot playing at, making friends and influencing people? This could be the end of the Firm as we know it. Bloody hell!"

Prince Philip is 94.

DAILY TELEGRAPH | Friday, 23 March 2012

Letters to the Editor

SIR – The wearing of the cross has been one of the proudest traditions of Christian Englishmen (and indeed women) ever since the days of the Crusades. No one was offended then, and the recent edict of the National Health Service that no one can be allowed to wear a hot cross bun in hospital wards is surely a sign that we are now living under a reign of intolerance reminiscent of the worst days of the Emperor Diocletian.

Though in the past I have not customarily worn a hot cross bun in my lapel to my workplace, I can assure your readers that, had I not been in retirement for 25 years, I would be doing so next Monday morning as a gesture of defiance to all these do-gooding busybodies who would curtail our ancient freedoms.

George Herbert Gussett (no relation)
Gerrards Cross, Bucks.

SIR – As ever, the commentators have missed the key point about the laws making wearing a cross a criminal offence. This is that the ban derives from our friends in Brussels, namely EU directive 2004/79 which outlaws the wearing of jewellery likely to incite religious or racial hatred.

They have further reinforced this outrageous infringement of personal liberty by way of the EU's Health and Safety in the Workplace directive 90/271 which lays down that employees may not wear any metallic accessories likely to put the health and safety of their colleagues at "material risk".

I would recommend the nurse who has been sacked for her "offence" under these laws to join the only party which is dedicated to freeing Britain from the shackles of this Brussels dictatorship, ie UKIP.
Rev. C.J. Barkworth
Monbiot St George, Somerset.

SIR – I am sure that all your readers who saw the case of that poor nurse with the crucifix will have been as "cross" as I was.
Mike Giggler
Via email.

SHOCK REPORT SAYS NURSES SHOULD CARE FOR PATIENTS

by Our Medical Staff **Florence Nightnurse**

BRITAIN's nurses were yesterday up in arms after a shock new report recommended that nurses should show "compassion" to their patients rather than calling them "love" or "dear".

The report, produced by various under-employed and over-paid senior NHS managers with nothing better to do, found to their amazement that a top priority for nurses should be attending to their patients' needs rather than filling in paperwork and ignoring old ladies who want a drink of water in the middle of the night.

"Our researches have shown," the report states, "that one of the prime tasks of care profes-sionals should be to care for those in their care."

The report reserves special criticism for the practice of addressing elderly patients with such dismissive and derogatory terms as "dearie", "pet", "chuck" and "Mrs Jenkins".

CAREMONGERING

"The correct terminology," the report concludes, "for conducting an appropriate nurse-patient verbal interface should be centred on such formulations as 'Stop whingeing, you old bag, it's not my job to keep running around after smelly geriatrics like you. I've got a degree, you know, so I'd shut up if you know what's good for you'."

(Is this right? Ed.)

Fallen angels

"I'm afraid the nurse can't 'have a chat' with you until she's completed the 'effective communication with patients' module of her course"

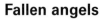

'Shaken judges' scandal grows

BY OUR FAMILY COURT STAFF CAMILLA CAVENDISH-SQUARE

A NUMBER of senior members of the judiciary have shockingly been diagnosed as suffering from "Shaken Judge Syndrome" or (SJS), after realising that they had been responsible for appalling miscarriages of justice in the family courts.

The judges in question had previously been perfectly happy to order children to be removed from their parents on the basis of "expert" evidence that parents "must definitely have been abusing their kids because it stands to reason".

When it was revealed that these experts had never met anyone involved in the cases, and were being paid thousands of pounds by social workers for producing nonsensical reports, one judge, Lord Justice Harvey Wallbanger, said, "We are all shaken to death by these terrible revelations.

"These so-called experts are clearly guilty of abusing the judiciary and should be removed from their families at once, for this is the only language such people understand".

"Of course, she's had a lot of work done..."

1952 SIXTY YEARS AGO

How the Eye gave a heartwarming tribute to the late King George VI

PRIVATE EYE

KING'S LAST SPEECH

I'm d-d-d-d-dead

Genuine facsimile copy of the magazine from 1952

The Alternative Rocky Horror Service Book

No. 94 A Service for the Expulsion of the Anti-Moneylenders from the Temple.

The President: Depart in peace.

Unhappy Campers: Do we have to?

The President: Look, it's nothing to do with us. As you know, we are totally behind you and we would be quite happy for you to stay as long as you like, but in a very real sense, you have to go.

Campers: That's such a shame.

(At this point, a procession of police officers shall enter the precincts of St Paul's Cathedral armed with riot shields and prepared to manhandle the congregation off the premises)

The President: Before you go, would you like to listen to a sermon from our former colleague, the Rev. Giles Spart, who is now a columnist on The Guardian newspaper?

Canon Fired: You know, in a real sense, this is the age of politics as mimesis... Shelley's Mask of Anarchy... Peterloo Massacre... what would Jesus do?... you are many, they are few what a scorcher... *(continues for several hours while congregation is peacefully removed)*

The President: Let us thank God they've gone!

Tourists *(from outside the Church)*: Can we come in again now?

The President: Open thou our doors.

Tourists: Do we really have to pay £15 a head to get in?

The Dismissal with Faint Praise

The President: You know, they meant well and we had a lot of sympathy for what they stood for, but in the end, frankly, it all got a bit embarrassing.

(At this point, the tills of the Cathedral will ring out to celebrate the return of business as usual)

© CofE 2012

New stamps unveiled: Great Daylight Robberies

Dick Turpin

The Great Train Robbers

The Brink's-Mat Gang

60p for a First Class Stamp

ROYAL MAIL SAYS, 'WE'LL SOON BE BACK IN PROFIT'

*by Our Postal Staff, **Gavin Stamp** and **Janet Once-Daley-Mail***

IN a dramatic bid to restore the fortunes of Britain's ailing postal service, the Royal Mail plans to increase the price of a first-class stamp to £5 billion.

"We recognise that this is likely to reduce the volume of postal items entering the system," announced the managing director of the Royal Mail, Moya Greed, last night, "but if only one letter gets sent at the new tariff, this should put us back in profit. This will allow us once again to take pride in a great British institution which has long been the envy of the world, so that

we can flog it off to a foreign buyer as soon as possible."

When challenged about the Royal Mail's controversial plans she said, "I haven't had a single letter of complaint. This shows that the public are entirely on our side. Or possibly that the sackful of letters dumped down by the railway embankment was actually for me."

When our reporter called Ms Greed, she initially said that she was out so we left a card inviting her round to our inconveniently located office between the hours of 9.30 and 10.00 (not Saturdays).

THE MARIE COLVIN I KNEW

BY PHIL SPACE

WHEN I heard the news that one of the world's most fearless, beloved and brilliant journalists, Marie Colvin, had been killed in Homs I was gripped by a sadness which I'd never experienced in over 20 years as a journalist.

Why?

I was sad because, as far as I could recall, I'd never met the woman and I knew that at any minute my editor would email me, asking me to bash out 5,000 words about my close friend, Marie, detailing our friendship... how much Marie valued my wise counsel... how she treasured the times we shared together... the laughs and the tears as the bullets whizzed around our ears...

And then it struck me. We had met. Marie and I had once sat three tables away from each other at some dreary awards do in 2006 – a night where I got terribly smashed and threw up over Eve Pollard and Marie won something for being a great journalist. So I realised that I could probably stretch this to a few thousand words about myself with a bit about her and (cont. 94 pages)

NEW HARRY POTTER THEME PARK

Expensiamus!

SARK SPRING
The World Watches

by Our Political Staff SAKI

Channel Islands, Tuesday

A MASS demonstration numbering tens of people gathered yesterday on the island of Sark to express opposition to the hated dictatorship of the ruling Barclay family.

The brothers, Sir Gilbert and Sir George Barclay, own large amounts of the island, including hotels, businesses and the propaganda sheet *The Sarky Newsletter*.

The twin despots live in a luxurious palace on the tiny fortified island of Brilleau, which has its own pad for helicopters. Their paternalistic regime has become hugely unpopular amongst the people of Sark, who are now calling for "an end to the Barclays' tyranny".

The Barclay brothers recently introduced elections to the island, but were humiliated when their candidates were defeated. They have now retreated into their bunker and are ignoring the demands of the electorate.

Observers are worried that things could turn nasty, with demonstrators being bombarded with unsold copies of the *Daily Telegraph*, which (cont. p. 94)

TOO OLD TO WRITE ABOUT MADONNA?

By Phillipa Space

Sitting at my computer preparing to knock out 5,000 words about how ridiculous Madonna looked at 53 in skin-tight fishnets, I was suddenly gripped with a dread thought:

Am I too old to write about Madonna being too old to wear skin-tight fishnets?

I then remembered how, as a youthful 23-year-old, I'd knocked out 5,000 word articles about how empowering it was to see a 23-year-old Madonna proudly commanding the stage in skin-tight fishnets, with no effort at all, and I still had the energy to party all night and shag into the early hours.

I remembered how, as a still youthful 33-year-old mum, I'd knocked out a 5,000-word article saying how envious I was at how great Madonna still looked in skin-tight fishnets, as I was picking up toys from the floor and feeling the odd twinge. I even recalled how, as an exhausted 43-year-old mum of three, I dragged myself to the end of a 5,000-word piece saying that at 43 surely it was time for Madonna to think about hanging up the fishnets…

Inappropriate outfit **Appropriate outfit**

And now here I was, at 53 still churning out articles about Madonna's inappropriately skimpy costumes.

Was this even an appropriate subject for a 53-year-old? Shouldn't I be writing that book I always said I'd write? But then I remembered just how expensive the children's university fees were and I realised that you're never too old to tell Madonna that she's far too old. *(Cont. for 5,000 words.)*

I absolutely ADORE understatement

ME TOO!! I completely bloody love it

Coming soon to a Gnomeon near you

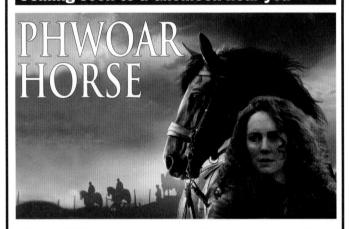

PHWOAR HORSE

TEAR-JERKING new film about the life of police horse, Bung, who falls into the hands of cruel, flame-haired Rebekah, and is taken into the heart of the circulation war where millions are lost on a daily basis.

Riding into the fray, Bung endures the mud slinging, the sniping and the appalling battles where men lose their sons (James) in an afternoon of carnage.

Don't miss the popular charge scene where Rebekah is charged following a dawn raid and accused of taking Bung. You will laugh, you will cry with laughter, as "Phwoar Horse" brilliantly recreates the insane decisions of the idiot high command fighting to regain a tiny patch of land from the Daily Mirror. In the end poor Bung is lent to dashing old Etonian Captain Cameron, who promises to look after the horse but instead returns Bung in a shocking condition cut to pieces and half strangled with red tape, fit only to be sent to the Inspector Knacker's Yard, from where he originally came.

But in a surprise happy ending, Bung leaps over the barbed wire at Wapping and escapes to see out his days giving evidence to the Leveson inquiry.

Based on an untrue story from Chief Inspector Michael Mormunyo, after he was given £10,000 in an envelope over lunch.

With acknowledgements to the lucrative puppet show "Pisspoor Horse", in which Sun journalists manipulate politicians to do whatever they want.

CAST IN FULL

Rebekah Brooks...............**MERYL STREEP**
Bung The Horse...........**REBEKAH BROOKS**
David Cameron...**BENEDICT CUMBERPATCH**
Rupert Murdoch........**VINCENT PRICE-WAR**

★ Nominated for ten convictions and lots of Laftas *(That is enough. Ed.)*

★ The producers would like to assure the public that no celebrities were hurt in the making of this film, though Steve Coogan felt a bit upset *(I said that's enough. Ed.)*

"Told you so," **The Guardian**

"Not us," **The Mail**

"Evil," **Empire**

"......" **The News of the World**

47

DIARY

ROD LIDDLE

Sitting on a train the other day, with my flies wide open so as to allow a nice bit of fresh air to circulate, I was roundly upbraided for my action by a red-faced Guardian-reading halfwit, apparently convinced that no one wanted to take a gander at my John Thomas.

You couldn't make it up. Whatever happened to good manners?

I told this smug, self-satisfied berk in no uncertain terms that many a fair maiden, and a sprinkling of old poofs, too, would pay good money to get an eyeful of my wotsit, and here I was, giving it to them for free.

Sadly, I didn't have my Taser with me, or I'd have shot him a quick one between the ears. But the sad truth is that even if I'd succeeded in downing him, there'd have been no end of other leftie killjoys to take his place.

Wherever you go these days, it's always the same. You take your cock out for a bit of a breather, and all hell breaks loose. Blimey O'Reilly, the way some people get steamed up about it, it's as though you'd committed some sort of crime!

William Shakespeare. Could someone please tell me what all the fuss is about?

Sadly the simple act of being a man is fast becoming a criminal offence in this nanny state of ours.

Time was when our forefathers were not only allowed but actively encouraged to walk down the street as nature intended. But now you only have to take out your dick and waggle it outside a shop window and the forces of political correctness are down on you like a ton of bricks.

And, believe me, I speak from experience. Just this week I was walking along Oxford Street. It was a pleasantly sunny day (so much for the fat-cat prophets of climate change industry!) and the shop windows were giving off a very clear reflection.

Well, I'm a man, and I make no apology for it, regardless of the howls of rage it may provoke from the hairy-browed, caber-throwing Lesbian community.

As a man, I reserve my inalienable right to take a good long peep at my meat-and-two-veg wherever I bloody well want. And if it's in the reflection of the front window of Top Shop, well, so much the better.

Ambulances. Who needs them?

The smug Stalinist brigade at the BMA – and don't get me started on THEM – are always going on at us blokes about the need to examine ourselves for prostate cancer and how we must all be open and straightforward and oh-so-21st-century about it, blah blah blah.

But the second we take them at their word and give ourselves a thorough going-over in the reflection of the Top Shop window, what happens?

Well, I'll tell you what happens, since you're asking. From inside the shop come the girlish screams and high-pitched hollerings of the wilfully female. And from outside the shop, up minces a motley assortment of the limp-wristed, air-kissing bouffant-haired luvvies who now constitute Her Majesty's Police Force. And before I know what is happening, they're forcing me to put it back in against my will and I'm being frog-marched, Nazi-style, to the nearest Cop Shop.

One minute, you're out enjoying the sunshine, the next you're being subjected to merciless strong-arm tactics from the ooh-get-you bully-boys of the Met. It's the kind of fascistic behaviour that Robert Mugabe himself might applaud. And don't get me started on Robert Mugabe!

I'm at a loss. Could someone please tell me what Norwegian serial killer Anders Brevik actually did wrong?

So I'm released without charge. Is that really the best they can do? If they want to give you a slap on the wrists these days, that's all they do – they release you without charge!

But it's not over yet. Not by a long chalk. Later in the day, I found myself the subject of an even more intense hammering from the stop-that-at-once brigade.

And this time what had I done wrong? What abominable crime against humanity had I been found guilty of by the monstrous regiment of nosy-parkers?

Right first time.

Smoking. An innocent ciggie. And in a park, of all places! So now you're not even allowed to smoke in a park!

So there I was, enjoying a quick puff in Hyde Park when an uppity Park Warden marched up to me like a tin-pot Hitler and told me to stop what I was doing.

"So now we're not even allowed to smoke in a park!" I said.

"Not without your trousers and pants on, you're not" he replied.

And they call this a free country! Police state, more like!

As told to CRAIG BROWN

CHELTENHAM CLAIMS MORE VICTIMS
Lame Nags Put Down

IN THE worst week of casualties in the history of the Cheltenham Festival, race-goers were shocked to witness the spectacular fall of a number of unthoroughbreds who then had to be put out of their (and our) misery.

Those Fallers In Full

Ginger Lady
Rupert's Boy
For Neville
Digger's Folly
Desert Coulson
Cameron's Fury
Eton Mess
Knacker's Yard

What are the odds on us going to jail?

INACCESSIBLE TOILET →

ACCESSIBLE TOILET

K.J.Lamb

NEVER TOO OLD

A new love story by Dame Sylvie Krin, author of
Heir of Sorrows and *Duchess of Hearts*

THE STORY SO FAR: Ageing tycoon Rupert Murdoch has been on the defensive as his empire has been racked by scandal. But now he is fighting back...

IN his luxurious penthouse suite on the 94th floor of the Newscorp Building in Manhattan a reinvigorated Rupert Murdoch chuckled as he read the front page of his UK quality tabloid *The Currant Bunday Times*.

The headline screamed out, "Cameron humiliated in Dinner for Donors Sensation".

"That'll teach those toffee-nosed pommie bastards to give me the cold shoulder," he crowed. "No one is going to say that Rupert Murdoch is past it!"

"You just said that, old man," retorted his young bride from the Land of the Great Paywall of China. "You lepeating yourself, Lupert."

"Fair dinkum, Wends," agreed the as yet non-nonogenarian media mogul, "but I'll tell you one thing. No one is going to say that Rupert Murdoch is past it."

Wendi sighed and let the matter drop. She had not seen her husband so happy and so full of zest in years. He was like a man of 75 again. Why ruin his moment of triumph? she thought, as she returned to her martial arts practise, throwing a six-blade star, the traditional Ninja weapon used against Ginja assassins which then embedded itself in the red-headed cardboard target marked "Lebekah" next to the recycling bin.

Rupert barely noticed in his resurgent delight in the power of his worldwide organs.

"Now for some tweeting," he cackled, as he started to punch in 140 characters of solid score-settling. His lips moved as his fingers pounded the buttons of the little black device...

"Ha bloody ha... Great scoop... Cameron's a dingo's arsehole... Trust must be established... Full enquiry... Importance of democracy..."

Wendi listened in growing disbelief. "You make complete twitter of self! You never heard of word ilony?"

However, Rupert was unstoppable. "'Fraid I haven't, my little terrorcutie warrior! But believe me, Revenge is Tweet."

And with that bon-mot he punched the button to send but, to his surprise, rather than his message being conveyed around the twittersphere, the giant 140-inch Panicson plasma television screen sprang to life.

"That not your phone, Lupert: that TV remote control!"

"Ah, Jeez, easy mistake to make," mumbled Rupert. He threw aside his state-of-the-art RottenApple iPhoney, as the screen filled with the hated logo of the BBC worldwide news and the announcer gleefully began a summary of the main headlines again:

"More trouble for Rupert Murdoch as the police in both the United Kingdom and in America investigate new illegal hacking claims."

The octogenarian shook his fist at the plump, orange-faced newscaster. "Bloody pinko, Guardian-reading Huw Edwards," he shouted. "Vengeance will be mine! I'll get you all! I know where the bodies are buried."

"Yeah, the same place you going, old man, if you don't calm down!" she soothed, passing him a tepid cup of Complete Horlicks.

Out across the Manhattan skyline the low rumble of a gathering storm sent a tremor through the ancient skyscraper.

(To be continued...)

GLENDA SLAGG

The Thirst Lady of Fleet Street!! (Geddit??)

■ SO SIMON Cowell's *not* gay!?!! Pull the other one Mr so-called biographer!? Apparently super straight Simon had all-night bonkathons with Dannii, Kylie, Cheryl, Natalia, and every other gorgeous gal who has ever been on telly!! Now, we're told he's the raunchy romeo with the sex factor?!? (Geddit??!!) Girls *allowed* (geddit!?!) Britain's Got Totty *(yes, all right, Ed.)* Do we believe this for a second!?! It's a "no" from me, Simon!!?

■ SIMON Cowell – he's not gay!?! Auntie Glenda with her infallible gaydar knew it all along!?! He's had everyone from Dannii Minogue and SuBo to the Queen (and I don't mean Louis Walsh!!?) Now, every red-blooded gal in the country has a chance of taming sizzling sex-bomb Simon!!? At last the truth is out – unlike Simon!?!! He's more hunk than monk – although he does have a Cowell?!?! Geddit!?? *(This is terrible, Ed.)* Does this little lady fancy joining the steamy list of the Cowell conquests!? It's a yes from me, Simon !?!!

■ NIGELLA – what a cheapskate!?!! Fancy flogging your best friend's book on ebay when she had signed it just for you!? Domestic goddess!! If you want to be careful with the pounds, don't eat so many chocolate cakes!?? (Geddit!!)

■ HATS OFF to Nigella!?! So she flogged off some boring old book written by a so-called friend who then blabbed all on the Twittersphere!?! Why shouldn't a gal be careful with the pounds!!? Even one as svelte as Nigella after eating all those chocolate cakes!!? So stop whining whoever you are and leave our Nigella alone with her cakes!?? *(You're fired, Ed.)*

Byeee!!

CRAZED WOMAN FOUND IN COWELL'S HOME

Poor Simon had to hide in the closet...

The woman's been detained under the Mental Health Act...

...and will appear on the final of Britain's Got Talent in two weeks' time

"Quiet tonight"

Han-z-z-zard

Budget statement 12.00

The Chancellor of the Exchequer, The Rt Hon George Osborne *(Tatty, Con)*: May I begin by congratulating myself on guiding the economy to a more successful state than it ever reached under the previous government.

(Tory cheers)

I am proud to announce that we have achieved a record level of government spending.

(Tory and Lib Dem cheers)

I can today inform this House that, under this government, the United Kingdom has recorded the largest figure for our national debt in history, over £1 trillion pounds.

(More cheers)

Furthermore, we are now well on course to reach a total of £1.4 trillion by the end of this Parliament. I am sure the House will agree that this is an achievement worthy of being recorded in the history books. In order to achieve this, of course, we will have to continue to borrow at an unprecedented level. In February alone, I managed to borrow £15 billion, or £3.5 billion every week. This is no easy task, but as a government we are committed to taking difficult decisions to borrow very large sums of money in order to carry on spending at a record rate of which I think we can all be proud.

(Labour cries of "Shame")

Before I commend this "Budget for Debt" to the House *(Tory laughter)*, I should perhaps add that there are a few other measures which you will already have read about in the newspapers, thanks to my Lib Dem colleagues.

(Lib Dem cheers, Tory boos)

Let me just list them quickly, because they are rather technical. I am cutting the top rate of tax by 5 percent.

(Wild Tory cheers)

I am simplifying pensioners' allowances with special reference to the payments to grandparents.

(Silence as MPs try to work out what this is about)

I am further imposing VAT on all hot pasties until they have cooled down to room temperature, in which case no VAT will be charged.

(Cornish MPs boo)

I am also adding £10 to the price of a packet of cigarettes, £20 to the cost of a six-pack of supermarket beer and £1,000 to the cost of taking a family on a cheap package holiday to Florida.

(Whole House boos. Mr Eric Joyce, Gorbals, Independent, Ex-Lab, head-butts all other Members within reach)

All this is necessary, as I am sure the House will agree, to ensure that both our spending and taxes continue to rise, and that we remain firmly on course to achieve a level of national debt that makes us the envy of Europe and will help to reassure the international markets that we are not just on a par with our Greek partners, but actually outstripping them. I commend this Budget to the House.

(Coalition Members wave order papers hysterically)

The Speaker, Mr John Berk: Order, order. I cannot allow Members of this House to cheer Government spokesmen. I call on Mr Ed Balls to restore a little balance to this farrago of nonsense from Mr Osborne, by replying for the Opposition. You may now cheer.

(Labour Members cheer, apart from the Rt Hon Edward Miliband)

Rt Hon Ed Balls *(Morelies, Alloutwood, Lab)*: This is the most disgraceful Budget speech I have ever heard. All this Chancellor has done is to impose a savage cut in the rate at which our national debt is increasing.

(Labour cheers)

A measly £1 trillion is all he can offer us. I can tell this House that, under Labour, this figure would have risen a lot faster and a lot higher.

(Wild Labour cheers)

Having robbed the nation's grannies in order to reward his fat-cat banker mates, no wonder he's looking so "pasty-faced".

(Hysterical Labour laughter in response to amusing play on words with reference to well-known West Country regional food item)

Rt Hon Nick Clegg *(Deputy Prime Minister)*: I would just like to

(House empties)

Why Even I Think Cameron Has Lost The Common Touch

by Charles Moore

I regret to report that the events of the past week have shown that the Conservative leadership is sadly removed from the everyday experiences of the average Briton such as myself.

Mr Cameron's lamentable ignorance about the exact whereabouts of pasty emporia only demonstrates that he is living in a cosseted, cocooned environment far away from the gritty reality of life as lived by those of us in the modern world.

Had Mr Cameron had an advisor such as myself, someone with his finger more closely placed on the national pulse, he would not have made such a string of schoolboy errors.

For his information, pasties are readily available from any Fortnum & Mason's hamper above the bargain price of £785. And Fortnum's is, of course, conveniently located just across the road from "Heffers", the purveyors of quality silk top hats to the gentry about whom I have written once or twice before in this column.

Furthermore, the solution to the supposed petroleum crisis is very simple. Forego the automobile and get on one's horse!

That way, one can cock a snook at the bully-boy tactics of the trade unionists without the public thinking that you are in some way a so-called "toff".

CAMERON'S FALSE CLAIM SHOCK

by our Political Staff **Simon 'The Pieman' Hoggart**

THE Prime Minister's credibility fell to a new low last night after claims that he had enjoyed a pasty bought from West Cornwall Pasty Company outlet in Leeds.

It has now been revealed that the place he bought the pasty closed down several years ago.

Said a spokesman, "Leeds was officially shut down in 2008."

The Prime Minister's office subsequently qualified Mr Cameron's original claim, "It may not have been Leeds specifically but it was definitely somewhere in the North."

However, the CBI confirmed that this was extremely unlikely since the North had been closed down since 1984.

Mrs Thatcher is 94.

CAMERON CRACKDOWN ON CHEAP BOOZE

From now on, it's £250,000 to have a drink with me

BIG BROTHER CONTESTANT WINS BY-ELECTION

I'm going back into the House

How humiliating

DINNERSFORDONORSGATE DAY 95

'NO INFLUENCE GAINED AT NO. 10 DINNERS' — Shock New Claim

by Our Political Staff **Phil Coffers**

A REGULAR attendee at the Prime Minister's Downing Street kitchen suppers has vigorously denied that personal access results in any sort of influence over government policy.

He said, "I've tried very hard to change the Prime Minister's mind, but it has never made any difference."

Mr Clegg, who wished to remain anonymous, continued, "Look, I've paid a very high price to sit at the PM's table and, believe me, I've got nothing in return. Not a sausage. Ok, possibly a sausage."

The Prime Minister's office responded to Mr Clegg's latest intervention. "Mr Clegg is entitled to his opinions but, frankly, they are of no interest to us."

When pressed for a personal reply from the Prime Minister himself, Mr Cameron later said, "Nick, can you pipe down, clear the table and get on with the washing up".

Guardian By-Election Round-up

Editorial Why this result has nothing to do with Muslims **2**

Opinion Why do awful people go on about this result having something to do with Muslims? by Libby Glibb **3**

Comment It was the Muslims wot won it by Mehdi Hassan *(surely shome mishtake)* **4**

On other pages The Rev Giles Flannel on his new parish of St David-the-Spart in Neasden **94**

 Dave Snooty AND HIS NEW PAYPALS

DONOR IS SERVED !

VERY GOOD CRUDDAS

WHAT'S THE SEATING PLAN, SAM CAM ?

IT GOES FAT CAT SLEAZEBAG, FAT CAT SLEAZEBAG...

I SAY - IS PUBLIC SERVICE INCLUDED ?

IS THAT A GONG ?

NO, THAT COSTS MORE !

INVITE TO BLANK CHEQUERS PBAB

IT'S PBAB READERS - PLEASE BRING A BUNG !

Why I hate all this sunshine

By Max Hastings

IF ONE more idiot has the audacity to say to me "Isn't it a lovely day?", I shall literally throttle him with my bare hands.

No, it isn't a lovely day. It's a national disaster.

Week after week the sun blazes remorselessly down on the parched fields and empty reservoirs of a Britain that is dying for lack of water.

How dare all these stupid and irresponsible people wander around saying "Good morning" to each other as though we were not facing a catastrophe of biblical proportions.

Only last week I was standing in one of our most celebrated trout streams, trying to catch a fish, when I suddenly realised that there was no water in the river and that my new green Hunters were as dry as a bone.

This is just one example of how this unprecented drought is threatening to wipe out our national way of life.

When is the government going to wake up and take the drastic action we need to save us before it is too late?

Here are just some of the measures that I have read about on Wikipedia before writing this article *(Surely "spoken to many of Britain's leading hydrological experts"? P.D.)*:

● It should become compulsory to put a brick into every lavatory cistern. This would save an estimated 2,000 billion litres of water a year.

● It should become a criminal offence for anyone to run a bath more than 15mm deep (except in Scotland).

● All Britain's roads and pavements should be dug up, to allow rain to seep naturally into the earth, thus refreshing our sorely tested aquifers. This measure alone could conserve a quantity of water equivalent to 500 million swimming pools.

● A new law should be introduced today to criminalise the use of such phrases as "Turned out nice again", "Don't the daffodils look lovely in the sunshine?" or "Weren't we lucky with the weather for our charity walk?".

Anyone found guilty of making such offensively droughtist remarks should be subject to a summary fine of £5,000 – which is what the editor offered me when he rang up this morning to say "Lovely day, Max, could you do us one of your brilliant pieces about this wonderful weather we're having?".

North Korea To Receive 240,000 Tons of Food Aid

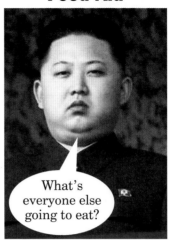

What's everyone else going to eat?

"Customers who bought this item also bought speed, crack, smack, blow and weed"

NUMBER OF QUANGOS SLASHED FROM 512 TO 896

by Our Cuts Staff **Peter O'Bore**

AN inquiry by the Public Accounts Committee into QUANGONE, the body set up to reduce inefficiency and waste in quasi-autonomous non-governmental organisations, has found that the cost of reducing expenditure on quangos has trebled in the past six months alone.

QUANGONE (mission statement *"Say Goodbye to Unwanted Quangos"*) had recommended the closure of 506 quangos, at a saving of £3bn. It now emerges that, while it wasn't looking, another 384 quangos had been set up, at an additional cost to the taxpayer of £48bn.

Last Quango in Matthew Paris

The 48 members of the QUANGONE board (average salary £186,000 a year for a two-day week, excluding holidays and the Olympic period) were last night quick to defend their record.

The board's chairman Sir Tim E. Server last night pointed out, "It is jolly hard to keep up with these quango fellows. They seem to work on a kind of 'close down one, get two new ones free' basis.

"If we're going to get on top of this problem of totally unnecessary and overstaffed quangos, then we need several thousand more staff on very much larger salaries who are here on the sharp end trying to cut down all this waste and inefficiency.

"We reckon that for a mere £180bn, we could have a real bonfire of the quangos, cutting their numbers down even further from the current 915 (it's already risen by 19 since you started reading this article) to a much more manageable 1505."

The Adventures of Mr Milibean

Fountain & Jamieson

CAMERON IS A DISGRACE!

HAVING HIS BIG DONORS FOR DINNER!

IT'S COMPLETELY OPPOSITE TO THE WAY I DO THINGS AS LABOUR LEADER...

...WHERE THE DONORS HAVE **ME** FOR BREAKFAST!

UNITE STRIKE

HEY, I'VE JUST FOUND A BIT OF PASTY! RESULT!

ORANGES

HENRY DAVIES

TEACHERS PROTEST AT HAVING TO TEACH CHILDREN TO READ

by Our Education Staff **Michael Whiteboard**

BRITAIN'S top teaching union, NOTREAD (the National Organisation of Teaching Representatives, Educationalists and Deputies) last night voted unanimously to go on strike against government plans to force them to teach pupils to read and write before they leave school at 16.

Said union leader Phil Literate, "It is an outrage and a total attack on the professionalism of teachers everywhere to suggest that they are in some way failing because so many children finish their education without the totally obsolete and outmoded so-called skill of being able to read."

The Phonic War

The Department of Education denied that they were trying to undermine teachers.

Said the Secretary of State, Michael Gove, "All we are doing is bringing in a test for 5-year-olds in which they have to show they are capable of reading a passage from the Guardian in which all the letters have been jumbled up so that word recognition alone can enable them to decipher the meaning of what Mr Rusbridger has been writing."

"My uncle got a promotion. He's my dad now"

CHILDREN'S TV STARS IN DRUG SHAME

By Our Media Staff **Andy Pandy Marr**

THE stars of some of the BBC's most loved children's shows have been revealed to have indulged off-camera in a drug-fuelled hedonistic lifestyle that would have shocked their young viewers.

Flowerpot men Bill and Ben were apparently "very fond of weed", which is why they talked gibberish all the time, merely saying, "Flobalob! Flobalobalob", to each other for long periods of time.

Also the popular horse puppet Muffin was exposed as a "drug mule" working as a courier to the so-called "Wacky-Baccy Races".

Said a BBC spokesman, "It is extremely regrettable that some of our children's favourites were behaving in such an inappropriate way, but we are pleased to announce that 'Looby Loo' is recovering in rehab after her experiences with super-strength skunk."

EYE POLL RESULTS

DOES THE LOW TURN-OUT IN THE RECENT LOCAL ELECTIONS MATTER?

Yes	2%
No	1%

WHY DO OTHER BRICKS HATE ME FOR BEING SUCH A BEAUTIFUL BRICK?

By Samantha Brick

I AM a young and very attractive brick and I often find myself in the company of a lot of plain bricks who are jealous of my looks and petrified that I will come between them and the building materials closest to them. And, let's be honest, every brick wants to be on top of me and not the other plain bricks. So why do other bricks hate me and accuse me of simply wanting to get laid?

 **Another brick responds**

WHO does this brick think she is? I consider myself a reasonably attractive looking brick but have the modesty not to go on about how well I get on with other bricks. Honestly, how insensitive can you get, you ugly lump!

 **Yet another brick responds to the other brick**

HOW can the other brick be so cruel? Shouldn't we all feel sorry for Samantha Brick and not pick on her obvious weakness, ie she is as thick as a brick, and between you and me looks a bit on the heavy side.

 **Another brick spots the Brick Bandwagon and responds to yet another brick's response**

WHY are the newspapers filling their pages with all this nonsense about bricks? Have we bricks got nothing more important to think about than how we look? Have we forgotten that our fellow bricks are being thrown in Athens, in Madrid and, yes, in Homs? We should all feel ashamed of ourselves for being distracted by one stupid, insignificant, half-baked brick who would be lucky to be picked up by a short-sighted builder's mate.

● *For more pictures of unattractive bricks, see my wall on UglyFacebook.*

"Not too much off the back!"

No. 94 George Osborne's Remarkable Finding

AFTER Newton and the apple and Humphry Davy and his canary, the discovery made by George Osborne in 2012 ranks among the most memorable in Britain's history.

George, an amateur economist, was sitting at dinner one day with some of his very rich friends when the conversation turned to the subject of taxation, which was one of George's interests.

"When there are so many rich people in England," remarked George, "I can never understand why the government can't raise enough money in tax."

"Good heavens," exclaimed one of the multi-millionaires sitting next to him. "Don't you realise, George, that rich people like us don't pay any taxes?"

A hearty guffaw ran round the table, as all the other diners chipped in to express their astonishment at George's naivete.

"Surely you realise, Osborne, that all of us very rich people have a little man who ensures that we never pay a penny in taxes?"

How they all laughed! But George had the last laugh. He went away and wrote the paper which we now know as 'Osborne's First Law of Taxation', in which he explains that rich people don't pay taxes.

It was published in the Daily Telegraph in April 2012 and is now widely considered to be one of the greatest contributions to human knowledge since Heisenberg's Principle of Uncertainty, as it affects death and taxation.

"I'd suggest tightening his belt, but then I'm an economist"

DOUBLE-DRIP RECESSION

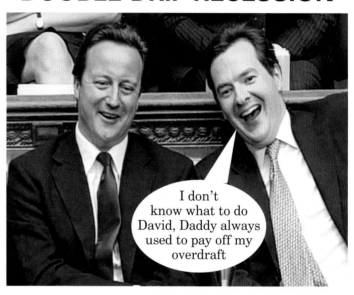

I don't know what to do David, Daddy always used to pay off my overdraft

George Osborne's week

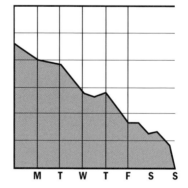

M T W T F S S

Black Monday

Blacker Tuesday

Blacker still Wednesday

The Blackest ever Thursday

How Black can Black get Friday

Hooray it's Saturday

Oh no, it's one day to Black Death Monday Sunday

Next week: *The same only more Black*

Daily Mail
COMMENT

Shame Of European Court Of Human Rights

TODAY we condemn the European Court of Human Rights unreservedly for its ruling that the UK is able to deport Abu Hamza to the United States.

How dare this hated court deliver a ruling which makes common sense and, even more disturbingly, we agree with?

How are we supposed to condemn it as a sham kangaroo court, saddling Britain with its ludicrous judgments upholding the human rights of terrorist scum, when it makes reasonable decisions like this?

We demand that the court returns to making crackpot judgments immediately so we never again find ourselves in the insidious position of having to agree with one of its rulings.

Letters to the Editor

Boat Race Terrorism

SIR – In common I am sure with all your other readers, I was utterly disgusted by the interruption of this year's Oxford and Cambridge Boat Race by a self-styled political protestor. Did this thoroughly irresponsible young man not realise that the Boat Race is one of our most cherished national sporting events and that his reckless action spoiled the pleasure of millions of viewers (quite apart from allowing the clearly inferior Cambridge crew to snatch a wholly undeserved victory!)?

In my view it would have been preferable for the Oxford crew simply to have rowed on, even if this led to the unfortunate decapitation of the hapless demonstrator. Did this foolish young man not realise that, by his pathetic anti-social behaviour, he brought whatever political cause he stands for into total disrepute?

Sir Herbert Gusset
(Pembroke, Oxford, Fifth Eight 1926).

The Guardian Friday April 20 2012

Letters and emails

Boat Race Heroism

In common I am sure with all your other readers, I was hugely impressed by the imaginative, non-violent way in which the Boat Race protestor chose to put across his very important and timely political message, ie that elitism as exemplified by the sickening antics of a tiny privileged minority of students who can afford to spend their time rowing around the upper-class suburbs of West London leads to the police state being imposed by the neo-liberal public school educated fascists of the Cameronist-Cleggite Coalition to create a country where legitimate protest is outlawed and you cannot even swim in the Thames without getting arrested.

Dave Spart
(Co-Chair of the Keep Qatada in Britain and Free the Boat Race One Rainbow Socialist Alliance).

DOWNSTREAM ABBO

After the triumph of 'Titanic', JULIAN FELLOWES tackles the second most disastrous aquatic disaster in living memory

Scene: The banks of the River Thames, sometime in the early 21st century. A plucky Oxford rowing team are powering their way through the misted waters, moving their paddle things backwards and forwards.

Butler: Will you be wanting Pimms on the upper deck, Ms Cox?

Cox: Not now, Carson. I have to stay alert. Disaster may strike at any commercial break.

Rowing person: Careful to avoid the banks, Ms Cox! There are ordinary people in these waters!

Cox: I don't think we need to worry, number one. In these early days of the 21st century, some time after the Iraq war and in the second year of the Conservative-Liberal Democratic coalition government, I hardly think we're going to collide with commoners!

Man from bank: Trenton! Trenton! TRENTON! Jesus Christ! Trenton!

Close up on half-submerged commoner (can we give him a hat with corks on it?)

Australian: Down with stuff, such as the beautiful timelessness of British life and the glorious pomp of the royal majesty!

Cox: Hard to porch! Splice the banjo! Curve the ligature!

Montage of panic and confusion. Various flunkies emerge from the lower decks and throw sandbags and croquet mallets at the Australian. The boat finally negotiates its way past the submerged colonial and toots in triumph.

Cox: I see what you mean number one. There are common people in these waters.

Rowing person: He was not what I was referring to, captain. I believe there are people from Cambridge University in the vicinity.

Cox: Good God!

Montage of terrible collision. Everyone drowns, or gets wet, or something. Then the whole incident is replayed from the point of view of Carson, the Australian, a duck, and the BAFTA judging panel.

TV Ratings go down with all hams (Surely "hands", Ed.)

From The Message Boards

Members of the online community respond to the major issues of the day...

TV bosses drop survivalist

Guys, have you heard about Bear Grylls? Discovery Channel has cancelled the new series. Mrs B is inconsolable! – **Bogbrush**

I am an animal lover but I haven't heard of bear grills before. If it involves mistreating bears for human entertainment then there is ABSOLUTELY NO PLACE FOR IT on our screens. – **Lassie_Louise**

Don't worry Louise, the only "bear" who suffers is Bear Grylls! He's an army officer who had a serious back injury and became a survivalist who eats insects and drinks his own urine! – **Bogbrush**

i suvive on chip's and tost but i never drink urin exept the time i founed some – **colin**

bear shithouse is a bellend who stays in hotel's when he claim's to be livin in the wild 😠 come to stoke and weel see how hard u are posh boy – **stokie_steve**

This business about his staying in hotels has been blown out of all proportion. What about those soldiers on the survival exercise in Wales? It turned out they had checked into local hostelries at night. Bear is ex-SAS so he was probably employing basic training methods! – **Robert "R"**

I would rather sleep in a sheep dip than in a Welsh hotel. – **Seb**

Fuss about nothing. Ditto the urine. I played rugger for forty years and downing the odd pint of piss was the least of your worries – **Zicka_Zimba**

Don't know if Bear plays rugby but he sure is SCRUMmy! And an Etonian too! I dread to think what would happen to his bad back if I got my mitts on him! 😊 – **Tilly**

ot bein funny but u sure he is etonian? theres load's of them round here and they cant hardly speak english at all. most of them are cleaner's and bilder's – **Hayley_321**

fair play to bear he was an SAS rupert and he was injured but he battled his demon's and bounced back. with all due respect to myself ive been there and when i talk to Andy McNab, Chris Ryan and other ex service guy's we can relate to bear so fair play – **Bravo_2_Zero**

hey bravozorro remind me agen wich service u serv in? the only uniform i seen u in was the postel service when u was deliverin my letter's LOL u was injurd by a gate and ur survivel method is sicknes compo from the post office LOL give my regard's to ur mate's chris and andy next time you stork them at a book signe-ing LOL – **Cherry_boy**

no sign of bear here wat a fuckin surprise 😏 soft twat – **stokie_steve**

NEVER TOO OLD

A new love story by Dame Sylvie Krin, author of
Heir of Sorrows and *Duchess of Hearts*

THE STORY SO FAR: Media mogul Rupert Murdoch has been called in front of the feared Leveson Inquiry. Now read on...

"WOULD you like to take the oath, Mr Murdoch?" The silky smooth tones of the judicial enquiry's top interrogator, Robert Jaycloth QC, put the octogenerian tycoon at his ease, and Rupert felt his confidence return.

"I swear… I swear to get my revenge on all the bloody bastards who have ever got in the way of Rupert Digger Murdoch. So help me, God. And God help them."

"A somewhat unconventional oath," interjected Lord Levesonandon, the wise judge presiding over the inquiry, "but we will accept it in this exceptional case."

And so it began, the great Inquisition that Rupert had feared would have him grilled like a jumbo prawn on a Bondi Beach barbie in the sizzling Sydney heat. But somehow, instead of being relentlessly and cruelly skewered by a razor-sharp fork, Rupert found himself being gently prodded and basted in oily politeness by the English legal system's finest.

He started to bat away the questions like Donald Bradman facing the pisspoor pommie bowling back in the good old days.

Phone-hacking? "No, don't recall a thing." Four!

B-Sky-B? "No idea what you're talking about, sport." Six!

Harry Evans? "Lying little lickspittle. Just like Andrew Neil and Gordon Brown and Colin Myler and Uncle Tom Croney and all." Double six again!!!

The aged oligarch from Oz felt a youthful adrenalin surging through his veins. Gone was the shambling, senile old has-been of previous appearances. Here was a fit, feisty, 81-year-old at the peak of his powers.

He looked across at his beloved Wendi, sitting poised like a crouching tiger or a hidden dragon ready to defend him against any pie-wielding assailant. He winked at her. That potion she had put in his prune juice this morning certainly seemed to be working! What was it again? Powdered panda glands mixed with ground spermwhale horn and concentrated dodo DNA…

Strewth! No wonder he was making mincemeat of the bearded barrister.

"I always say that revenge is a satellite dish best served cold, if you get my meaning."

The loud laughter of his newly-favoured son Lachlan filled the courtroom.

"Bonzer banter, Pops! And whatever else you forget, *don't* forget to give me the whole company in your will!"

Rupert smiled proudly. "That's my boy!"

And on and on it went, as Murdoch senior settled scores by the score and avenged the injustices of his hundred-year career.

Major, Brown, Cameron… he swatted them all like so many flies gathering round the rotting corpse of a dead koala underneath the kulabar tree.

But this cuddly old bear was not dead by any means. No, siree!

"No, I've never asked a pommie prime minister for anything," he deftly responded to yet another slow full toss on leg stump from Mr Jaycloth, QC, "There was no need.

The spineless bastards always gave it to me on a plate."

"Ha, ha, ha!" Lachlan's loyal laughter rang out again, telling the world that the mighty Murdochs were not finished yet – except for James of course.

"My son Jimbo is, I'm afraid, a little inexperienced." Rupert put on the humble face that he had been practising for months with his trusty legal advisers Pantson, Fire and Partners.

"In fact, when it comes to crisis management I'm afraid Jimbo is about as much use as a vegetarian dingo in a baby-eating contest."

There was a shocked silence in court punctuated by Lord Levesonandon coughing. "Yes, I think that's all we have time for. You must be very tired, Mr Murdoch, and we're very grateful to you for giving us so much of your very valuable time."

And with that his ordeal was suddenly over and he felt an overwhelming tiredness overcome his weary frame as his eyelids drooped…

RUPERT woke suddenly to the shrill sound of his SamCamSung mobile phone alarm playing the opening bars of Rolf Harris' classic hit, "Two Little Posh Boys".

He turned to his beautiful, somnolent bride from the land of Lap Sang Su Bo.

"Jeez, Wendi, I had the most amazing dream. I went to the inquiry, got an easy ride, dished the dirt and single-handedly brought down the government."

"It no dream, old man. It leality!"

"You mean…?" stammered Rupert.

"That what happened."

"But I don't remember…"

"No! No! Inquiry finished now, Lupert! You don't have to keep acting."

"But I really have no recall of…"

"Time for more prune potion, Grandad. This time double strength…"

And as Wendi turned to the chest full of traditional Chinese medicines, Rupert felt his euphoria drain away and somehow the taste of revenge in his mouth was less sweet than sour… *(To be continued...)*

ME AND MY SPOON

THIS WEEK

TAKI THEODORACOPULOS

Do you have any favourite spoons?

I like all types of spoon, except black ones.

NEXT WEEK: *Jean Marie Le Pen, "Me and My Pen".*

LONDON MAYOR 2012

'TOO CLOSE TO CARE'

by Fraser Nelsons-Column

AS THE two main contenders for London's top job, and the other ones as well, made their final appeal to Londoners to wake up, a poll commissioned by YouBore revealed that Ken Livingstone and Boris Johnson are now polling the same high level of indifference.

An astonishing 94% of Londoners really didn't give a monkey's which of the candidates won. The rest were less bothered. Said one man on the doorstep, "Go away. I'm not in."

However, there is still time for the contenders to swing the voter (Sid Bonkers) their way.

The Mayor, Boris Johnson, was however keen to emphasise the difference between himself and Mr Livingstone. He told Radio Neasden's popular 4am Snooze Time Phone-In, hosted by legendary DJ Colin Snooze, "The thing is, old bean, that Ken is a fucking liar, whereas I am... an Old Etonian."

How they stand on the key issues

BORIS	KEN
Cheaper transport	Transport that is cheaper
Freeze on Council Tax	Council Tax frozen
More bobbies on beat	Beat to have more bobbies
Sunshine for Olympics	Olympics to have sunshine
An end to personality politics	Personality politics to be ended
Another four years	Four years more

THE EYE'S MOST READ STORIES

Cameron stands firm

Despite rumblings on the backbenches, the Prime Minister promised that he wouldn't be backing away • from controversial reforms of the House of Commons that would see the number of

Liberal Democrat MPs after the next election reduced to zero.

"For too long Liberal Democrats have thought they have some God-given right to have some MPs, but as the local elections showed, that's no longer the case.

"This matters because it's an issue dear to the heart of the ordinary Tory voter in the street planning to vote UKIP at the next election."

Nursery Times

Friday, April 27, 2012

Family Court Removes Children From Parents After Pail Of Water Incident

by Our Court Staff

A BROTHER and sister, J and J, were yesterday forcibly removed from their parents' home by 18 Toytown police officers and the team leader of the Nurseryland Social Services Department, Ms Snow Queen.

Their removal followed a report that the two children had been slightly injured when they fell down a hill near their home, where they had been sent by their parents to collect a pail of water.

As they descended from the well, two "falling incidents" occurred in quick succession, as first Child J tumbled to the ground, quickly followed by his sister Child J.

Well, well, well

After J had returned home from hospital after being treated for a suspected "broken crown", paediatricians alerted social services, who immediately summoned PC Plod and his colleagues to take the children into foster care.

Said Ms Queen last night, "The parents of these two children deliberately exposed them to the risk of serious physical and emotional harm by allowing them to go up the hill with a bucket in a wholly

unsupervised water-fetching situation.

"Such callous disregard for the children's safety is clear evidence of neglect. We had no option but to apply to the courts for an emergency care order."

This was immediately supported by Lord Justice Humpty Dumpty, who said, "I have never seen a more shocking case of child abuse than this horrifying tale of two children being deliberately thrown down a well by their sadistic parents."

The children, J and J, were last night reported by Ms Queen to be "very happy in their new home, the Gingerbread House, being looked after, along with Child H and Child G, by one of our most experienced foster-witches."

● **Late News** *Foster-witch burned to death in oven shock: children blamed.*

Pooh Sticks Race Ruined By Protestor p. 2

Captain Hook Extradited To Never Never Land p. 3

Dick Whittington Tells Mayor Rival "You're a F**king Rat". p. 94

POETRY CORNER

In Memoriam
Kim Jong-il,
North Korean Leader

So. Farewell
Then
Kim Jong-
Il.

You were
Kim Jong-
Il.

Then you were
Kim Jong-
Very-il.

Now you are
Kim Jong-
Dead.

> E.J. Thribb (17½)
> *PS. Keith says/"A grieving nation/*
> *will all sing/'We're So Ronery'."*

In Memoriam
Davy Jones, 1945-2012

So. Farewell
Then
Davy Jones.

Former lead
Singer of the
Monkees.

Yes,
You have taken
The last train
To Clarksville.

And,
Hey, hey, you are
No longer a
Monkee walking
Down the street.

I wonder
If
You are now
A believer.

> E.J. Thribb (17½ rpm)

In Memoriam
Robin Gibb, of the
popular singing group
The Bee Gees

So. Farewell
Then
Robin Gibb.

"Tragedy".
Yes, indeed.

"Staying Alive".
Sadly not.

"Too Much Heaven".
We do hope
So.

> B.G. Thribb (33⅓)

FIRST DRAFTS

Rachel Cusk

Ian McEwan

Kathy Reichs

Max Hastings

In Memoriam
Vidal Sassoon
Hairdresser to the stars

So. Farewell
Then
Vidal Sassoon.

"Going away
Anywhere nice
On holiday?"

Yes, that was
Your catch phrase.

Now your life
Has been
Cut short.

And you
Have gone away on
The final holiday of all
Somewhere nice.

> E.J. Thribb (17½)

In Memoriam Eugene
Polley, inventor of
the television remote
control

So. Farewell
Then
Eugene Polley.

Inventor of the device
That has changed
All our lives.

Without you
We would still have
To get up
From the sofa,
Walk across the room
And change channels
Manually.

Now, alas, you
Have been
Switched off.

> E.J. Thribb
> (Channel 17½)

In Memoriam
Philip Gould, architect of
New Labour

So. Farewell
Then
Philip Gould.

PR man extraordinaire and
Supreme Spin
Doctor to the
"Blair Project".

Your final achievement
Was to organise
Every detail of
Your own funeral.

Which means that
You were literally
"Spinning in your
Grave".

> E.J. Thribb (17½)

That Nationwide Olympic Torch Relay In Full ⚬⚬⚬⚬⚬

Day 94 The Flame Reaches Neasden

Sally Sooper: And welcome back to "Good Morning, Dollis Hill", your favourite BBC Neasden breakfast show. And there's only one thing of any importance happening in the world today and that's the Olympic flame coming right here to Neasden.

Remember, this sacred flame has already travelled 200,000 miles, all the way from Mount Olympus in Greece, on an incredible journey which has taken it from Lands End to John O' Groats, from Billericay to Belfast, from Littlehampton to Llanfairpwllgwyngyllgogerychwyrndrobwllllantysiliogogogoch.

And now, unbelievably, it is just about to arrive in Pricerite Road, Neasden, where our reporter Jilly Gosh is interviewing the youngest of all the 450,000 heroes who have already carried the torch the length and breadth of Britain, from Lands End to John O' Groats *(voice in earpiece says, "We've done this bit, Sally")*. So, Chantelle Chatterjee, you're only three-years old and you have been selected from everyone in your primary school for the huge honour of carrying the Olympic flame 20 metres down Pricerite Road. How do you feel about this extraordinary privilege of taking your place in history as the youngest person ever to carry the Olympic flame on its way to the new Olympic stadium to launch the biggest sporting event the world has

ever known? *(Jilly's question is so long that Chantelle has already begun her epic 20-metre walk down Pricerite Road to hand over the flame to the next torchbearer)*

Jilly: I'm afraid we seem to have lost Chantelle there. I think her parents are already off to sell her torch for 25p on eBay, so if you want a souvenir of this amazing and historic event, you'd better start bidding now.

Meanwhile I'm just pushing my way through this vast crowd of an estimated 200,000 people to speak to the next torchbearer, 93-year-old Second World War veteran, former Colour Sergeant Ghurkali Lumleywallah, who has recently settled here in Tesco Road, Neasden.

Sergeant Ghurkali, how does it feel to be taking part in this extraordinary journey of the Olympic flame on its sacred and utterly historic journey all the way from ancient Greece to the Neasden of today? *(Sergeant Ghurkali's carer has to point out that his wheelchair has already disappeared round the corner into Poundstretcher Avenue)*

Jilly: So, incredible scenes here, Sally, but for the moment it's back to your studio for a full summary of this morning's astonishing scenes as the Olympic flame finally reaches the familiar streets of Neasden and Dollis Hill, on its way to *(cont. for 94 days)*

ASSANGE SEEKS ASYLUM IN UGANDA

by Our Political Staff **Jonathan WikiLeake**

THE international dissident and founder of WikiLeaks, Julian Assange, has tonight sought refuge in the Ugandan Embassy.

His supporters confirmed, "Julian **is** currently discussing Uganda in the ambassadorial spare room. He has always loved Uganda and greatly admires the Ugandan way of doing things."

Assange, who was due to be extradited to Sweden, has formally appealed to become a Ugandan though, at present, it is uncertain whether the Ugandan Embassy has given its consent to Mr Assange's unexpected entry. Said a spokesman, Jemima Khanihavemymoneyback, "I'm sure this affair won't last long – Julian doesn't like to take no for an answer."

Rochdale Police Entry Exam

1. Study the above picture. Can you spot any similarity between these eight convicted sex offenders?

a) They are all white   **b)** They are all women   **c)** Don't know

The correct answer is c). If you haven't a clue, you should apply to Rochdale Police at once (or Rochdale Social Services or the Crown Prosecution Service).

School news

....

St Crumpet's (Leading Independent School for Girls)

Headmistress: Dr Helen Righton

Kardashian Term ends today. There are 1,742 girls in the school. Ms D.V.D. Sex-Tape (Kims) is Head of Reality. Ms I.V.A. Big-Butt (Loadeds) is Keeper of the Nuts.

The House Thong contest will be held in Strippers' Hall on July 7th.

A careers talk will be given by Ms Katie Price (OC) in the old Library on the subject of "Fags, Shags and Wags".

There will be a performance of the musical "All That Vajazz!!" by the Sixth Form in the Revue Bar on July 28th. Tickets from the Bursar Mr Dirty Desmond.

Role Models have been cancelled.

Sexeats are on Nov 7th.

UK AREAS AT RISK OF FLOODING IN FULL

Possible flood areas marked in blue

"OK. Let's really raise the roof with this one!"

Enoch was right about everything

By C. Moore, S. Heffer and A. Cabbie

IT MAY not be fashionable to say so, but on the centenary of the birth of Enoch Powell, we believe it is time to reassess the legacy of one of Britain's most controversial politicians.

In the light of how history has unfolded since his death, we can see that Enoch was not merely the finest orator since Demosthenes but the most prescient politician of all time.

Here are just some of the issues on which Enoch has been proved dramatically right:

● His prediction that the EU was not a very good idea and would end in tears

● His insistence that when governments spend more than they receive in taxes it can only end in tears

● His firm view as an Ulster Unionist MP that there could never be any reconciliation between the Protestant and Catholic communities in Northern Ireland

● His conviction that all scholars would one day agree that Shakespeare could never have written St John's Gospel

● His prophecy that the River Tiber would foam with much blood, in which he has been fully vindicated by history – except that he possibly didn't get the name of the river right. It was the Thames.

© Charles 'Charlie Boy' Moore, Simon 'the Heff' Heffer and Ted Snozzer, Cab No. 666

Notes & queries

Where does the word 'chillax' come from?

● "Chillax" is not, as the Reverend Sally Strepsil fancifully claims, an abbreviation of the phrase "Chinese laxative", an oriental bowel-loosening linctus given to British soldiers stationed in Shitzu Province during the Boxer Short Rebellion at the beginning of the 20th Century.

"Chillax" is, of course, a word of Indian origin, coming to English from the troubled province of Utter Rubbesh and was much used by the sepoys in the Indian Mutiny (now known as the War of Indian Independence). The local word for tea is "chai" and the Goddess of Good Fortune is "Lakshmi", so literally "chillax" came to mean "a lucky cuppa" and was known as the ideal way to relax after a busy day massacring British residents in the siege of Krishnan Guru-Murthy.
Rear Admiral Jilly Foghorn-Smythe, HMS Pinafore.

● The good lady Admiral is, of course, talking the sort of poppycock that one expects from a generation woefully unversed in the Classics.

As any Greek scholar will tell you, Chillax was the younger brother of Ajax, the famous hero warrior of Homer's Iliad. Whilst his brother was winning renown in the ten-year siege of Troy, Chillax stayed at home, drinking wine, playing games and singing songs on his *karaokes*, an early Greek musical instrument brought out at feasts, particularly in the brothers' birth place, the sleepy island of Dedlos.
Professor Mary Moustache, Morse College, Oxford.

Answers to the following please:

What is a Santander?
What is Pudsey's real name?
Why Bryony Gordon?

THEN AND NOW

I have nothing to offer but blood, sweat and tears...

1940

Anyone for tennis?

2012

 Dave Snooty AND HIS NEW PALS

I'M REALLY UNDER PRESSURE AT THE MOMENT - WITH EVERYONE TELLING ME I DON'T WORK HARD ENOUGH!

YOU NEED TO DO SOMETHING TO UNWIND, DAVE!

TENNIS?

ED BALLS PLEASE!

FRUIT NINJA?

DIE! DIE! DIE! SIMON HUGHES!

KARAOKE?

IT'S MY PARTY AND I'LL CRY IF I WANT TO

W'H'INE?

CLEGGIE IS SO USELESS!

NO - I'M GOING TO RELAX BY HAVING A BIT OF **SERIOUS** FUN...

I'M GOING TO **RUIN** EVERYTHING FOR WHEN **BORIS** TAKES OVER! HA! HA! HA!

NOW THAT'S WHAT I CALL **CHILLING**, EH. READERS?!?

QUEEN'S SPEECH

More austerity, I'm afraid

NEWS STORY NOT ABOUT TWITTER SHOCK

By Our Media Staff **Janet Tweet-Porter**

IN AN unprecedented piece of journalism yesterday, a national newspaper ran a story that had nothing to do with the social networking site, Twitter.

Said the editor, "I know it is unusual, but a real event happened in the real world and I thought I had an obligation to report on it. I apologise to readers if in this instance I got it right."

Reaction in the Twittersphere to the story that wasn't about Twitter was immediate and intense. Hundreds of thousands took to cyberspace to register their shock at what one typical tweeter called "lazy journalism".

Another tweeted, "Pathetic. Why can't they just trawl through celeb tweets and write it up like everyone else?"

@stephenfry joined in the debate responding to a tweet from @tomwatson who had retweeted a tweet from @rupertmurdoch criticising a tweet from @joeybarton commenting on @sallybercow's tweet which was picked up by @gracedent who was approving of @stephenfry's tweet about (cont. p. 94)

"Okay – who's the fish and who's the chicken?"

My Small Thin Greek Wedding

The fun starts as the latest round of austerity measures kicks in. The guests are told to bring their own food and not to break any plates because they are too expensive. Everyone cries.

Eye rating: Tragic

GREEK FASCISTS IN IRONY DEFICIT

We're not going to be told what to do by the Germans

"But I only ordered a medium!"

Euro 2012 Preview

Germany	**v**	**Greece**
Germany	**v**	**France**
Germany	**v**	**Spain**
Germany	**v**	**Italy**
Germany	**v**	**Portugal**
Germany	**v**	**Republic of Ireland**

Germany win on Financial Penalties

Tournament Slogan:
"They think it's über alles, it is now!"

FACEBUBBLE BURSTS

by Our South Sea Staff **Ivor Goodtip**

THE flotation of the exciting new social networking site, Facebubble, ran into immediate controversy last night when the shares in the company run by Mark Suckerberk dramatically plunged a bit, leaving investors slightly less rich than they had hoped.

Said one, "I wanted to make lots and lots of money. Imagine my disappointment and fury when I only made lots!"

Said another, "I have no idea how Facebubble works, but I think I should be given a huge amount of cash for doing nothing."

Said a third, "Look, I trusted Suckerberk, on the sound financial grounds that he wore a hoodie, looked about twelve and was in that film with Justin Timberlake."

Facecrook

Furious new shareholders were threatening to take Facebubble to court in order to get back the extra money that they didn't make when they made the first lot of money.

Meanwhile, the founder, whose personal fortune has now been reduced to a paltry 94 billion dollars, said, "I have suffered too. I have lost a lot of friends. But they weren't real friends. In fact, I never met most of them. My status remains 'Highly Enviable'."

"Beware of Geeks bearing gifts..."

The Timons of Athens

Friday June 1 2012

No End To Sisyphus Torment

BY OUR INTERNATIONAL EDITOR JOHN HOMER SIMPSON

THE Greek leader, Sisyphus, who has been struggling to meet his obligations of pushing a large boulder up a steep hill as punishment for squandering his country's fortunes, has been told that there is no respite in sight.

The Gods of the Market Place have told him that there is no help available to him and if he doesn't hurry up he will have to push an even larger boulder up an even steeper hill.

Sisyphus claimed yesterday, "This is an impossible task. Every time I get anywhere near the summit the rock rolls down and crushes me, making me even weaker and *(cont. until Grexit. Ed)*

"They just love winding up the neighbours"

SHORTAGES TO CONTINUE DESPITE RECORD FLOODS, SAY WATER CHIEFS

by Our Water Staff **Jonathan Leak**

THE bosses of Britain's privatised water companies last night warned that, despite the record deluge of money which has been flowing into their bank accounts, there is still not enough to meet their demands.

"It is inevitable," they said, "that our customers will have to pay very much more in future, because huge quantities of money keep leaking into our pockets and we are quite powerless to stop this."

Critics claim that the real problem facing the country is a shortage of water caused by the failure of the companies to build or maintain sufficient reservoirs to meet growing public needs.

A spokesman for the industry was, however, quick to rebut these claims. "It is not our job," he said, "to supply the public with water. Our chief concern is to ensure that there is a continuous flow of money into our wallets."

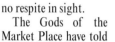

COMMENT

Protect Our Children From Online Filth

THERE was outrage today after a Google executive claimed there was nothing the company could do to shield children from degrading sexual imagery as they logged onto Mail Online.

"It is up to parents to keep their children away from disturbing images of Kim Kardashian flaunting her new gym-honed body on the beach in a skimpy bikini," said Naomi Gummer, "or Paris Hilton's topless Twitter pix."

In the past few days the Daily Mail has highlighted concerns over the ease at which children can access filth simply by clicking onto the Mail Online.

The Mail Says

TODAY we launch a campaign demanding an "opt in" policy that would mean users would be automatically blocked from visiting the Mail Online unless they specifically declared their wish to see Rihanna frolicking on a beach in an electric blue two-piece which leaves nothing to the imagination.

How long will we stand by and do nothing as the vile, salacious, Mail Online turns our nation's children into moronic sex-obsessed voyeurs?

 Dave Snooty AND HIS NEW PALS

SALEM WITCH TRIAL

DAY 94

by Our Crucible Staff ARTHUR MILLER

THE STORY SO FAR: It is New England in the Year of Our Lord 2012, and diabolical goings-on have led to the Witchfinder General being called in to determine who is guilty of bewitching whom. A simple girl, Rebekah, begins to denounce the good folk of the town.

Now read on...

Witchfinder (Mr Jay QC): Do not be afraid, child. Speak only the truth.

Rebekah: You've got to be kidding.

Witchfinder: Be serious, Rebekah – these are grave matters of good and evil and lives depend on your testimony.

Rebekah (*fiddles with her hair and tries to look innocent*): Yes, indeedy-do, sir, your honourship.

Witchfinder: Do you admit working as a minion for the Dark Lord?

Rebekah: I do, sir.

Witchfinder: And did you see anyone else consorting with the evil one?

Rebekah: Aye, sir, with my own two eyes. I did see Goody Cameron supping with the Beast on many occasions (*gasps of horror sweep through court as the reputation of an upright citizen is seriously impuned*).

Witchfinder: And what was the nature of Goody Cameron's dealings with the Devil?

Rebekah: The horned fiend wished to further his evil business upon the earth probably... I don't remember.

Witchfinder: Be careful of what you speak, girl.

Goody Cameron tells this court that you are betraying him because you loved him and he, to his shame, succumbed to temptation and loved you in return (*more gasps from court as extent of Hellish influence over country becomes clear*).

Rebekah (*as if possessed*): And it was not just Goody Cameron, sir, who danced with the Devil that night at the pyjama party – but Goody Osborne, too! He and Murdoch spoke privily in whispers.

Witchfinder: Heavens, child, where will this madness end?

Rebekah (*foaming at the mouth*): I denounce Goody Hunt, Goody Gove, Goody Brown, Goody Blair...

(*Hysterical screaming engulfs court-room as massed lawyers, scribes and townspeople pass out with excitement.*)

Judge Leveson: It seems to be that most of these Goodies aren't very goody at all – rather, they appear to be *baddies*.

Witchfinder: Very amusing, your honour.

Judge Leveson: Now, shall we burn the witch?!

All: Yeah!

(*To be continued*)

THE JOY OF TEXTS

What does LOL stand for?

Lots Of Lies!!

And what does DC stand for?

Nothing at all!

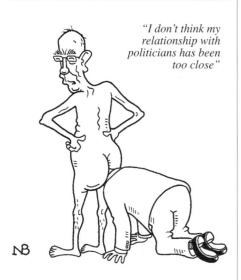

"I don't think my relationship with politicians has been too close"

NB

NUTTER DISRUPTS LEVESON INQUIRY

Hi, I'm Tony Blair...

Mary Ann Bighead

Ooh la large brain! You probably saw me looking sexy on the television and, if you didn't, here's a photo to remind you that I'm not just a very clever political commentator, but I'm also incredibly attractive and could pass for a saucy French maid, albeit one with a triple first in Advanced Brainology from Oxford College, Cambridge!

I was very cleverly doing a piece for the BBC about "cleaning up" Westminster. Did you see what I did there? I took the phrase "cleaning up" literally rather than metaphorically, thus cleverly illustrating what could have been rather a boring and not very clever piece about political ethics.

So in one fell swoop I showed I have top-rate analytical skills, a great sense of humour and a great pair of pins!

You could say that when it comes to being cleverer than everyone else, I "cleaned up"!

© Mary Ann Big Mistake.

The Eye's Controversial New Columnist

The columnist that demands to know who has taken his nose

I see that the so-called "great" British public are flocking to watch "The Bridge" on BBC4. Over one million viewers! This of course makes me very angry because I got into dark foreign thrillers years before everyone else, and naturally I never get the credit from the so-called "media" for being a trendsetter! I have been watching "The Garden" for ages now. It is a gripping foreign crime thriller in which two completely chalk-and-cheese detectives (Iggle Piggle and Upsy-Daisy) who don't speak a word of English investigate the low-life denizens of "The Garden" to discover who has taken Iggle Piggle's blanket. Two hundred episodes in and I am still hooked! (And there aren't even any subtitles to help.) It burst onto our screens in 2006, on the obscure arts channel CBeebies and, in my view, is far darker and even more interesting than the thriller that preceded it, "Tubbies", a gripping siege drama in which four desperate criminals kidnap children and hold them inside their stomachs *(cont. p. 94)*

Grey Matter

"Sorry, I'm a bit tied up at the moment"

"The great thing about the Kindle is that no one can tell what you're reading"

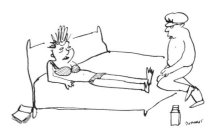

"You want to change your soap powder, love... those are a dreadful shade of grey..."

Fifty Shades of Earl Grey

Lovely tea Gladys!

tie me up in bondage and do me!

Kerber

Dirty Devil Flies In

by Our Man on Cloud Nine **Harp O'Marx**

The Devil continued his evidence today before the heavenly tribune presided over by Archangel Islington.

Questioned about his meetings with Mr Cameron, the Devil said he could not now recall how often they had met.

With his familiar goat-like features and shiny cranial horns the Devil seemed relaxed and at times almost genial for a man of 476,251.

"I have never sought to influence politicians in this way," he told the tribunal, "I have simply enjoyed meeting them and hearing their views."

Asked about his close relationship with the former German leader, Herr Hitler, the Devil said he had never tried to dictate his policies.

"We had many conversations," he said. "He was an amusing individual and I enjoyed his company. I am glad to say that I still see him on a regular basis."

The Devil was reminded that earlier he had given the tribunal a "solemn and binding undertaking" to tell the truth, the whole truth and nothing but the truth.

"Yes, I remember that," he said, "I have given a number of undertakings like that over the years. But I don't attach any importance to them. It's just a form of words. If that's what people want, then I'm happy to go along with it."

(The hearing continues)

'I AM NOT MAD'

Screams Brown

By Our Political Staff **Michael Whitecoats**

THE former Prime Minister, Mr Gordon Brown, yesterday responded to Rupert Murdoch's claims that he was "unbalanced" by shouting at a lamppost near his home.

He told the lamppost, "Me? Mad? Do I look like the sort of person who goes round shouting at lampposts? I bet you're working for Murdoch, aren't you? Well from now it's war with lampposts and all other public roadside lighting devices. Oi, you, post box, shut your big mouth!"

JEREMY HUNT CAUGHT ON CAMERA WITH MURDOCH CRONIES

New Oxford Dictionary

Hunt *(noun)* Slang. Highly derogatory. Term used to denote untrustworthy person with no loyalty to those working for him and an exaggerated respect for the rich and powerful. Can be used as compound *Total Hunt, Stupid Hunt* or, worst of all, *Jeremy Hunt*. From the anglo-saxon *Cnut* meaning one unable to turn back tide of sleaze.

What You Will Hear

The Archers Radio 4

(BBC cow mooing sound effect No. 1265)

Jill Archer: I'm slightly worried about the new boss, David. Apparently, he used to run Eastenders. *(Pause)* Are you alright, David? You seem to have shaved your head and burned the farm down for the insurance money...

David Archer: Leave it out, you slag!

Jill Archer: David! How dare you speak to your mother like that!

Ruth Archer: Oh, leave it out, you slag.

Jill Archer: Not you too, Ruth!

(BBC door opens sound effect No. 5678)

Jill: Everyone's acting very strangely, Clarrie. How's your day been?

Clarrie: Same old, same old. Me and Eddie murdered Brian Aldridge's cow and buried its body under the allotments. Joe had an affair with Mike Tucker's scarecrow, and then he helped us swap his baby for a pig. So, a pretty quiet day really!

David Archer: Leave it out, you slag!

Clarrie: Who's going to make me, you muppet?

Ruth Archer: Don't you call my David a muppet, you slag!

Clarrie: You want a piece of me? Yeah? You slag!

Ruth Archer: Bring it on, you slag!

David Archer: Fight... fight... fight...!

Jill Archer: Is anyone coming to the bring-and-buy sale at the church on Sunday?

All: Leave it out, you slag!

(Cont. for 987 episodes)

A victory message from the Mayor of London
Boris Johnson

What ho, Londoners! Bozza's back, bigtime! That was the message that went out loud and clear to the electors of Britain, when yours truly was returned to power in a stonking great landslide, with a monster majority of no less than 2 percent.

You know I'm not one to blow my own trumpet, but let's face it, I'm the only Tory in the whole of Europe who seems capable of winning an election at the moment.

And I did so against all the odds. Particularly when the lefties at the BBC, aka the Boris Bashing Corporation, decided to throw balance out the window and campaign openly for Red Ken! Cripes! The sooner we abolish them and hand the whole broadcasting caboodle over to my friend Mr Murdoch and his much maligned chums at BSkyB, aka Boris Sky Broadcasting, the better!

I even managed to overcome the not entirely welcome support given me by my old friend from school days and the varsity, Mr Cameron. No offence, Dave, just a bit of Bozza banter to show I've got a sense of humour. It's what the jolly old punters love about me, unlike certain other political leaders who can't take a joke and just go red in the face and start shouting at dotty women like "Sad Nad" Dorries and pensioners like poor old Mr Skinner. (No offence, Dave, but you've got to take these things on the chin – if you've got one!)

Anyway, let me make things crystal clear. Boris is perfectly happy to carry on making London the greatest city in the world for the next four years. There's no way I want my old friend Dave's job as prime minister, however many millions of people are suggesting that I should take over.

No way, Jose! Dave can rest assured that I am not going to add to all his problems by sticking my oar in on his patch and throwing my top hat into the ring at present.

I'll continue to cheer him on from the sidelines as he battles with the unholy shambles that he and his friend Nick are making of everything.

We can all see that the whole show is going to go tits up. (Excuse my French, ladies, just another bit of Bozza badinage to get the women's vote – who all prefer a loveable rotter to a dutiful stay-at-home bore – mentioning no names, but Dave may have some idea of my drift!)

So when the proverbial brown stuff hits the revolving air-conditioning unit, then the cry will go up "Send for Bozza!". It'll be just like the days when our Roman chums were absolutely desperate for someone to save their country when everything was falling apart. So they all went on bended knee to a chap called Cincinnatus, whom they'd previously thought was too posh for the top job, and the rest, my friends, was history.

So that's Boris's Latin lesson for the day. (I remember back at the old alma mater that "Dim Dave", as he was affectionately known to us scholars, was never much cop at Classics – nor, as we later found out, anything else!) But enough of all this. I'm off on my Boris bike to devote myself 100 percent to running London – until such time as my country calls me.

Your humble head honcho,

Borisius Cincinnatus Imperator

"We've closed the gap between rich and poor"

BBC Breakfast 'unaffected by location'

by *Our Media Staff*
Saul Ford

Sofa: happy to relocate

BBC bosses insisted yesterday that despite moving the morning breakfast show to Salford, the programme is "utterly unchanged".

Said a spokesman, "This is a slap in the face to all those critics who said the programme would get better. It remains as superficial as ever. It is a tribute to the professionalism of our presenters that they have managed to move to a brand new sofa and yet are continuing to deliver the same old (cont. p. 94)

EXCLUSIVE TO ALL PAPERS

WAS ENGLISH BUSINESSMAN POISONED OVER MULTI-MILLION POUND CORRUPTION SCANDAL AFTER AFFAIR WITH CHINESE LEADER'S WIFE?

● We've no idea.

THAT CHINESE DEAL MYSTERY SOLVED

Harro!

...and then Oxford!

Sorted!

How The Role Of The Queen Has Changed Over The Decades

50s | 60s | 70s

80s | 90s | Etc...

Friday
15 June
2012

theguardian

Britain Salutes 'National Icon of Dedication and Service'

by Our Media Royalty Staff
Michael Whitewash

For 60 years, this increasingly frail and isolated old lady has shown the people of Britain what it means to devote your life single-mindedly to public service and the good of humanity.

Year after year, however much the world has changed, she has stood steadfast and rock-like to the same basic principles.

People look to her to put over the same inspiring message week after week.

Ok, she's a little glum and people say she lacks a sense of humour.

But that is to miss the point of this iconic figure's role at the heart of British life.

She is there to remind us all that we are one nation – united in our support for the Labour Party, our contempt for the Monarchy and our firm conviction in everything that she and the Guardian stand for.

She is a very ordinary woman who has somehow made herself truly extraordinary.

So crucial a part of the fabric of our nation has she become that it is hard to imagine that when she is gone anyone could possibly replace her.

Never again will we see another Polly Toynbee.

© **The Grauniad 2012.**

GOD BLESS YOU, A.N. WILSON!
by HM Queen Elizabeth II

OLDER readers like me will doubtless remember the first glimpse we had of him. The black and white photograph in the Daily Telegraph showed a shy, donnish figure in a funny hat cycling through the streets of Oxford with a book of poems and a copy of the Spectator in his bike basket.

The nation was charmed by such a delightfully informal picture. Yet discerning readers could see on the features of that young man the unmistakable signs of courage, determination and a devotion to duty.

Prince Andrew Wilson

Never once in his long and busy career has A.N. Wilson shirked the call of duty – the duty to supply 700 or more words to fill up the leader page of the Daily Mail – "Save Our Beautiful

Then | **Now**

Bluebells", "Isn't Mrs Thatcher Ghastly?", "Isn't Mrs Thatcher Wonderful?".

He was willing to undertake any assignment, however ridiculous – his only reward, several hundred meagre pounds.

Now in this Jubilee Year he has produced a truly memorable tribute to myself, "I Salute You, Ma'am!", which shows that old-fashioned notions of chivalry and public service are still (cont. p. 94)

Pageant Organisers Promise Inquiry Into 'Mistreatment'

by Our Employment Staff **Stewart Ship**

ORGANISERS of the Royal Pageant have begun an investigation into claims an elderly couple were dropped off by car in Central London and then forced to stand on a barge for five hours in the pouring rain.

"We've seen plenty of examples of cruelty against the elderly, but this is perhaps the most shocking yet," said a disgusted Help the Aged spokesman.

Lovely Jubilee

"The taller one is now in hospital following the couple's brutal and inhumane treatment. They were too scared to speak out in case their state benefits were stopped."

A spokesman for the private security firm responsible blamed an administrative error for the mix-up, saying when the elderly couple arrived in London they should have been dumped under Blackfriars Bridge with the rest of the long-term unemployed working at the event.

AIR SHOW ↑

Daily Telegraph

Friday 15 June 2012

RAIN TURNS OUT IN FORCE FOR JUBILEE

By Royal Correspondent **Met Baker**

MILLIONS of loyal raindrops lined the sky yesterday to shower their support for the Queen's Diamond Jubilee.

Cynics had suggested that they wouldn't turn up and might be put off by the forecast of occasional sunshine.

But, instead, excited clouds gathered, many of them overnight, to release a tremendous outpouring of rain on the royal celebrations.

For she's a brolly good fellow

Said one raindrop, "I came all the way from the North Sea to be here. I wouldn't have missed the Queen for the world and, actually I didn't. I'm proud to say I caught her right on the head". He continued, "The atmosphere was very special – wonderfully damp right the way through the day".

From the lightest drizzle to the heaviest downpour there was no stopping the rain from making the whole event unforgettable.

Long to rain over us

Said another raindrop, "There wasn't a dry person in the crowd. I don't think I'm exaggerating to call this the biggest wash-out since the Coronation, when we *(cont. 94 inches of rain)*

On other pages

Will BBC coverage of Jubilee cause drop in house prices?

What you missed

To mark the Diamond Jubilee, the BBC is proud to present an exclusive documentary tribute by **His Royal Highness the Prince of Wales** to **Her Majesty the Queen**

Silly music. We see Prince Charles in the half-dark sitting by a dusty pile of old 8mm film cans.

Charles: You know, it's absolutely amazing, but these old home movies of my family haven't been seen for fifty years. Incredible, isn't it? Look at this one.

Cut to grainy black and white footage showing two small children playing on lawn with young woman in background.

Charles *(voice over)*: You see, that's me and Princess Anne when we were very young. And there, just coming into shot, is my Mama. You know, I find it tremendously fascinating. I expect the film was taken by my father. And look at this sequence shot a year or two later.

Cut to grainy colour footage showing two slightly older children playing on lawn with slightly older young woman in background.

Charles *(voice over)*: Now this really is extraordinary. That's me again, and my sister. And that's my Mama again. You know, children in our family have enjoyed playing on that lawn ever since the reign of Queen Victoria. I can't help suggesting that these amazing bits of film – which have never been seen before – convey the very real sense of continuity in our country's history. You see my Mama is Queen and one day, you know, I'll be the Kingie-thingie. And now here's another historic piece of film, from a few years later.

Cut to film showing small boy in cap and shorts going off to prep school.

Charles *(voice over)*: Oh look, there's me again. Isn't that rather wonderful? (*Charles's tribute to himself continues for some hours*)

Daily Mailograph

Friday 15 June 2012

Jubilee unites nation

By Our Couple On The Sofa **Anne and Bob Diamond**

AS the last cheers died away down the Mall and the sodden bunting was packed away to be tumble-dried ready for the Olympics, there was no doubt that the British nation had come together with one voice to say "We hate the BBC".

From the deepest Welsh valleys to the highest Scottish glens, from the clotted creameries of Cornwall to the call centres of Carlisle, from the wind farms of Wensleydale to the solar panel sales centres of Solihull *(Get on with it. Ed)*, our island race of loyal licence-fee payers chorused in patriotic unison, "Isn't Fearne Cotton useless?", "What was John Sergeant playing at?", "What has happened to Anneka Rice?", "What's on ITV? Oh look, there's David Starkey".

It was as though Britain was once again one nation, with no differences of class, creed or colour, unanimous in its common desire to see Director General Mark Thompson "strung up live on Sky or at the very least sent into permanent exile in Salford".

"Still nothing?"

Prince Charles An Apology

IN RECENT weeks and years and decades, in common with all other newspapers, we may have inadvertently given the impression that HRH Prince Charles was in some way unsuitable to succeed Her Majesty the Queen as the nation's monarch. Headlines such as *"Belt Up, Big Ears: We've Had Enough Hot Heir To The Throne"*, *"We'll Never Forgive You For Murdering Diana and Marrying Camilla"* and *"Make Wills King, Ma'am, and Skip The Prince of Loons"* may have led readers to believe that we felt that the normal principles of the hereditary monarchy should for some reason in this case be shelved on the grounds that Prince Charles was ill-equipped for the solemn and strenuous duties of kingship. We now realise that after he said "Mummy" and asked for "three cheers" for his father at a celebrity concert, Prince Charles is, in fact, the ideal successor to Queen Elizabeth II and indeed has all the qualities of wisdom, humility, patience and a thorough knowledge of both organic biscuit-making and the Goon shows which will undoubtedly enable him to become the most successful king since George VI. We hope our headline today will in some measure correct any misleading conclusions our less perspicacious readers may have drawn about our editorial position: *"Come On, Limpet Liz, Drop Dead And Give Bonnie Prince Charlie A Chance!"*. God save the King.

© *All newspapers.*

BBC COVERAGE OF THE FUNERAL OF HIS ROYAL MAJESTY DUKE PHILIP, PRINCE OF EDINBURGH

ALAN TITCHMARSH: Welcome one and all, wherever you may be, to this Right Royal Funeral here in the truly fabulous surroundings of St George's Chapel in the age-old city of Windsor. Well, the sun is shining and it's one heck of a beautiful day, but of course this isn't what one might call an altogether "sunny" occasion, is it, Sophie?

SOPHIE RAWORTH: Morning, Alan! There's a tremendous lot of excitement, with young and old come out to watch, and a group of kids by me painting lovely little miniature coffins, but, no, Alan, you're right – this is, at heart, a very very solemn occasion, as it's a funeral to mark the death of someone very, very special.

ALAN TITCHMARSH: Wonderful! And remind us who that very special person is, Sophie – or should I say "was"?!

SOPHIE RAWORTH: It's none other than His Royal Majesty Duke Philip, Prince of Edinburgh, Alan! For younger viewers, he's the one who was married to Queen Elizabeth 1 for I don't know how long! Years and years. But he's now, of course, very sadly died.

ALAN TITCHMARSH: Her Royal Majesty must feel his demise most terribly. How do you think she's feeling now, as she prepares for this, her big day, Sophie?

SOPHIE RAWORTH: They say she's very saddened by her husband's death, Alan – and who can blame her?! But it's worth remembering, Alan, that if he hadn't died, none of this would be happening today, and the whole event would probably have had to be cancelled, which would have been very disappointing, especially for all those who have come so far. So, in that sense, Alan, every cloud has a silver lining.

ALAN TITCHMARSH: So now let's go over to Dale Winton, with all the lovely people who've gathered outside Windsor Castle on this truly splendid occasion. What's the mood like down there, Dale?

DALE WINTON: Absolutely super, Alan! How are we all doing ladies? Give us a right royal cheer! Wooh! Yes! Well done, girls! They're all determined to have a really great time here today! And now back to you, Alan!

ALAN TITCHMARSH: I'm delighted to welcome Royal expert Simon Schama. Tell us something about King George's Chapel, Simon. It's something of an iconic building, am I right, Simon?

SIMON SCHAMA: Very much so, Alan. It has a history as long as my arm. It was in the 13th century that King Hen…

ALAN TITCHMARSH: Before you go all historical on us, Simon, I'm afraid I'm going to have to interrupt you because some sort of royal procession is now starting. So over to The Woman Who Knows – yes, it's our right royal fashion expert Eve Pollard, no less, soaking up the fabulous funeral fashion!

EVE POLLARD: Yes, Alan, the excitement's mounting as they're take their seats in King James's Chapel, which gives us a golden opportunity to take a look at their frocks! Sadly, the Royals seem to be playing very safe today. It's all black, black, black. Princess Kate is wearing black, and so's The Queen, who's the one in the centre, and even the lovely Pippa has opted for something very very dark. One longs for a flash of bright yellow or lime green to cheer up the proceedings! And what about showing a bit of leg for the blokes, Pippa?! Ha ha! Back to you, Alan!

ALAN TITCHMARSH: Thanks, Eve! And now we welcome the one and only Lord Andrew Lloyd Webber to the studio. A very sad day, then, in many ways, Andy?

ANDREW LLOYD WEBBER: Yes, Philip was a remarkable figure who came to see a great many of my shows – Superstar, Cats, Phantom – and he always took a keen interest in everything I was up to, so we'll all miss him terribly.

ALAN TITCHMARSH: And am I right in thinking, Andrew, that you have a brand new TV series on in the autumn?

ANDREW LLOYD WEBBER: Yes, we're all very excited, we'll be searching for the new Little Orphan Annie…

ALAN TITCHMARSH: I'm going to have to stop you, there, Andrew, as I'm being told something's happening in the Chapel. Talk us through it, Matt!

MATT BAKER: Well, Alan, this is very definitely the "Wow!" moment we've all been waiting for. Various military types, soldiers or sailors, I'd guess, are striding along holding what looks like a great big box on their shoulders...

ALAN TITCHMARSH: Might that be the coffin, Matt?

MATT BAKER: Hard to tell, Alan, as it's got a flag of some sort covering it.

ALAN TITCHMARSH: And what's the atmosphere like down there?

MATT BAKER: Not many smiles, to be honest, Alan! In fact, I'd almost describe it as funereal. Hang on, there's this bloke down the far end of the Chapel who's started to speak. I'm pretty sure it's Rolf Harris.

ALAN TITCHMARSH: No Royal occasion is complete without Rolf. Let's hope he'll sing Two Little Boys, in honour of poor Wills and Harry, who let's not forget have lost their dear old grand-dad…

SIMON SCHAMA: It looks to me more like the Archbishop of Canterbury, Alan.

ALAN TITCHMARSH: Oooh! Very POSH! Nothing but the best, eh? To get down to the nitty-gritty, Simon, I'd imagine he'd have cost the family rather more than some other vicars I could mention. But I guess he's worth it for all the dignity he offers, eh?

SIMON SCHAMA: I…

ALAN TITCHMARSH: Back to Matt in King John's Chapel itself. Well, the choir seems to be in full throttle, singing some sort of old and much-loved hymn, I'd imagine. Any sign of Gary Barlow, yet, Matt?

MATT BAKER: No, but once this is all over, I'll bet there's some mega celebs lined up for the after-party, Alan. With me now, as the coffin is carried back out, are Will. i. am, Ann Widdecombe, David Walliams, and Katie Price. Tell me, Katie – how well did you know Duke Philip?

KATIE PRICE: Who? Oh, him. He was well fit.

MATT BAKER: Could I ask you to speak up a bit, Katie? The choir's drowning us out! Back to you in the studio, Alan!

ALAN TITCHMARSH: A truly memorable day, a day most of us will probably remember for quite a few hours. So from the funeral of Prince George at St Philip's Chapel, Windsor, it's cheerio from us – and it's cheerio to him! Cheerio!

As told to CRAIG BROWN

ORANGE PRIZE 2012

Winner: Katie Price

"I understand it's not a happy ship"

WORLD'S DEEPEST HOLE FOUND

by Our Political Staff William Pitt the Deeper

It is being hailed as one of the most extraordinary natural phenomena discovered anywhere on earth.

At undisclosed locations extending across several countries between Greece and Portugal, evidence has been found to suggest that there exists a monster hole so deep that it is believed to be bottomless.

Experts say that, in a series of tests over the past four years, they have thrown immense quantities of money into the hole, none of which has ever been seen again.

Said Professor Kvantativ von Eassing, "We believe this hole is getting bigger all the time and that eventually the whole of Europe could fall into it – and possibly the rest of the world as well.

"But there is no cause for alarm," he continued. "We think we have found a solution to what we are calling 'The Euro-hole Question'.

"Even now we have factories in Germany constructing giant printing presses, so powerful that they will be able to churn out trillions and trillions of euro notes, in such quantities that we are confident that the hole can eventually be filled.

"Then," he concluded, with a triumphant cry, "we can all sleep peacefully in our beds for ever!

"Particularly," he added, "if ve hav taken ze precaution of stuffing a few gold bars under ze mattress. Ha ha ha! Who says ve Germans have not got a sense of humour?"

TIME FOR BRITAIN TO LEAVE EUROVISION?

by Our Political Entertainment Staff
Graham Naughtie and James Norton

THERE were growing calls last night for Britain to quit the European vision on the grounds that everyone hates us and we never get anything out of it.

This year the story was exactly the same as usual, with countries ganging up on Britain in order to humiliate the country's efforts.

One Eurovision sceptic complained, "The whole institution is flawed and the voting system is farcical. Everyone knows that it is entirely geared towards Germany.

"Few countries can afford the Eurovision any more and most are secretly desperate to get out of it. Greece, Portugal, Spain, Italy and even France are dying to make their exit."

Many years ago, the UK was a Eurovision winner with songs like *Congratulations Mrs Thatcher*, *Not a puppet on a string* and *Boomboomabust*.

But now we are reduced to being represented in Europe by has-been former stars like Williambert Haguedinck with his unpopular song *A referendum will set you free*.

MUSLIM BROTHERHOOD VICTORY

Will women have any freedom in the new Egypt?

I'm going to draw a veil over that

HISTORIC AGREEMENT REACHED AT RIO 2012

RIO+20

By Our Environmental Staff **Geoffrey Leanoverbackwardstotrytofindanythingpositivetosayaboutthistotalshambles**

WORLD LEADERS and Nick Clegg today concluded the most important earth summit since Rio 1992 by signing a truly remarkable Memorandum of Non-Agreement on all the problems confronting the world (except the Euro).

The document reads in full:

❶ 20 years ago the leaders of the world met in Rio to agree that something had to be done to save Planet Earth from imminent catastrophe.

❷ Among the problems they identified were the likelihood that unless immediate international action was taken, civilisation would soon be destroyed by melting ice caps, rising sea levels, unprecedented floods, droughts, heat waves, tornadoes, plagues, famines, wars and death.

❸ We accept that in the 20 years since that treaty was signed nothing at all has been done to avert these disasters.

❹ That is why we now all agree that it would be very nice if somebody would do something about all this, but preferably somebody else.

❺ We all have our own problems, let's be honest, and although we'd like to help, we agree with our Chinese friends who've got all the money, that all this environmental stuff can't be a priority at the moment.

Signed by all world leaders and, in the absence of David Cameron, Nick Clegg.

Gaia Man Apologises To The Planet

THE world famous environmentalist and visionary James Lovelock today told the Guardian that he had been "wrong about everything".

"How on earth could anyone even have believed all that rubbish about global warming, wind turbines and so forth?

"Believe me," he concluded, "it's all nonsense."

FOR SALE
HOUSE WITH CHARACTER

CAMERON'S PUB SHAME

I'm completely pixellated

Yeah, I've had a few too many as well

Child Abandoned

Social workers were called to a public house in Buckinghamshire to take an 8-year-old girl into care after her parents had abandoned her, as they heartlessly drove off home leaving the child sobbing alone.

A council spokesman said last night, "This is one of the most scandalous cases of parental neglect we have ever come across. We have applied for an emergency care order on Child N and she has been placed in foster care until we can find a new family to adopt her."

To protect the child, her parents cannot be named, but her father is believed to be a prime minister who lives with his wife in a country mansion near the village pub where the girl was abandoned.

Second Tory Pub Scandal

Eric Pickles has spoken of his distress and horror as, having left his local after a pub lunch, he realised he had accidently left a sausage on his plate.

"I thought it was being taken in the other car," said the distraught man mountain. "When I arrived home and realised it was still in the pub, you can imagine how terrified I felt.

"I immediately turned the car around and roared back. I was only gone fifteen minutes tops, but you hear all these horror stories about what can happen to unattended sausages.

"Fortunately, David Cameron's daughter happened to be helping out in the bar and she saved the sausage in a grease-proof box for me."

Rodin's 'Thinker, with Doer'

GLENDA SLAGG

The Queen of Tweet Street (Geddit?!?)

■ SHAME ON you, Dave and Samcam, for leaving your littl'un all alone in the pub after you've been a-boozin' and a-snoozin' over a liquid lunch!!? There's only one word for you two – you're an absolute disgrace?!! (*That's three. Ed.*) Forget Leveson, Mr and Mrs Prime Minister – you should resign now as parents!?!

■ SO DAVE and Samcam forgot little nipper Nancy down the pub for a few minutes while they were chillaxing with a drink or three!?! So what?? What parent hasn't driven off and left their kiddie behind without noticing??! For Gawd's sake, lighten up Mr Holier-Than-Thou Press Man!?! Dave and Samcam are just like the rest of us – stressed out after a tough week and in need of a right old knees-up in the local without worrying about the whereabouts of their screaming sprogs!!?

■ SHED A tear for poor old Damien Hirst!?!! He's the Brit Art Bad Boy who pickled a shark and put jewels on a skull!? Now his maverick missus has gone and ditched him for someone even more mercenary (Geddit?!?), ie Mr Wild Goose himself, Tim Spicer!!? Is that a gun in your pocket, Colonel, or are you just pleased to see her!?! (Geddit!!?) In this case, Damien, you're the one in a bit of a pickle because the <u>shark</u> has stuffed you!?! No offence!!?! Talk about a Broken Art (Geddit!?!)

■ SO DAMIEN Hirst's other half has done a runner with dishy dog of war Tim "Spicy" Spicer!?! And who can blame her!?! Who wouldn't trade in Deathly Damien's sicko sculptures of rotting sharks and rotten skulls (Geddit!!?) for an action man whose gun is loaded rather than his wallet??! Let's face it, Damien has made a bit of an Art of himself (Geddit?!!)

■ BEN GOLDSMITH!! You're the moping moneybags who's a-weepin' and a-wailin' cos your airhead heiress missus has ditched you for a raunchy rapper!!? (*Isn't this the same story again? Ed.*) OK, so it's a painful private matter with kiddies involved. But who cares? Let's all have a laugh at Bruiser Ben, Kallous Kate and Jay Electronica – crazy name, crazy people on Twitter!?!!

■ MADONNA!! Urgh!? So she's stripping off in Turkey!?! Put it away, Granny!?! Hasn't anyone told you, Madge, that the lads don't want you to get them out anymore!!? There comes a time for gals of a certain age to show some modesty – otherwise you end up making a right tit of yourself??! (Geddit?!!)

■ HATS AND bras off to the Queen of Pop!! Thank God that her Madgesty (Geddit?!!) has struck a blow in Turkey for all us gals of a certain age who still want to prove that they are not past it and aren't afraid to let it all hang out!! When it comes to flaunting your assets, Madonna, you're simply the breast (Geddit?!)

■ SALLY BERCOW!?! She's the Speaker's wife who called the jolly Jubilee fans "loonies" and then has the nerve to complain when people call her a silly cow married to a berk!?! Honestly, Mrs B, where's your sense of humour!!? Take a tip from Auntie G, love, "If you can't stand the tweet, get out of the kitchen!!" (Geddit??!)

Byeee!!

The Adventures of Mr Milibean

Fountain & Jamieson

YOU KNOW YOU'VE ARRIVED AS LEADER WHEN TONY BLAIR PHONES YOU!

YOU KNOW YOU'VE **REALLY** ARRIVED WHEN HE PHONES YOU REGULARLY!

AND YOU KNOW YOU'VE **REALLY REALLY** ARRIVED...

WHEN HE'S PHONED YOU MORE TIMES THAN HE DID GADDAFI!

ME   GADDAFI

HENRY DAVIES

What You Will See

THE THICK OF IT 2012

(Enter Malcolm Fucker, spin doctor to the Minister for Honours)

Fucker: This'll sort out the little Glaswegian gobshite.

Minister: Who?

Fucker: Armando fucking Iannucci, that's who! Thinks it fucking funny to make us look like a bunch of fucking foul-mouthed cunts *(camera wobbles)*.

Minister: So what are we going to do?

Fucker: We'll make the smug Scottish scumbag an offer he can't refuse.

(Jump cut to Minister's face)

Minister: I hope it doesn't involve violence?

Fucker: Only if we pin the fucking gong in his Eyetie eyeball...

Minister: Could you explain what you mean, Sir Humphrey?

Fucker: This isn't "Yes, Fucking Minister", you useless ball sack of democratically elected pus!

(Jump cut to wobbly camera)

We're going to give TV's Mr Satire an O Fucking B Fucking E.

Minister: Surely he'll never accept that. He's renowned for his lampooning of institutional establishment humbug and hypocrisy...

(Jump cut to wobbly minister)

Fucker: Of course he fucking will! He's more full of shite than the executive toilet in a Spanish bank...

Minister: But why **should** we give him an OBE? Services to comedy...? To broadcasting...?

Fucker: No. In order to make him look like a two-faced cunt.

Minister: That is really quite clever.

Fucker: Yes, I'm more fucking brilliant than a lightbulb stuck up Thomas Edison's arse!!

(Wobbly cut to jumpy minister)

Minister: Quite so. And one more thing, Mr Campbell, I mean, Mr Fucker. You must promise me that you will not put this fiendish OBE plot in your readable but unreliable diaries... You know, the ones you swore on oath that you would never publish?

Fucker: Yes, Fucking Minister.

EXCLUSIVE TO ALL PAPERS

FRUITY GIRLS SEEN IN MUD

by Our Music Staff
Heather Milling-About

THE Festival season threatened to be a washout, but luckily the arrival of some fruity girls in the mud prevented disaster as Fleet Street's middle-aged editors breathed a sigh of relief.

"If it hadn't been for the fruity girls in the mud, we would have had to run more pieces about the Eurozone with nothing fruity on the horizon until A-level results in August!"

Said one weatherman, "This year we have seen the highest levels of fruity girls in the mud since records *(cont. p. 94)*

(cont. p. 94)

QUEEN MEETS MARTIN McGUINNESS

And what do you do?

Nice hat, Ma'am

OK, CHERIE may have put her size 12 feet in it by attacking stay-at-home mums and calling them "Yummy Mummies"! It would be unfair to point out that Cherie may be a bit biased on this one due to her not being exactly "Yummy" herself (more "Gummy" in my book!). But she *does* have a point!!

POLLY FILLER
on Cherie Blair

Namely, that hard-working career women on the frontline of modern motherhood, walking the tightrope of work life balance and juggling the demands of family and employment are a damn sight better as role models for kids than the lazy, dependent, homebodies who sit around having coffee with each other, then go out drinking white wine in Maman's Bistro at lunchtime and end up watching Wimbledon all afternoon!!!

In the Filler household that is the Useless Simon's job! Real women go to work and their children respect them for it all the more.

My precious but deeply intuitive todder Charlie is always telling me, "Thank goodness you work so hard, Mummy. I really appreciate the fact that you don't come to any school events."

Bless him!! He's got the Filler feminist message already, ie all women should work, especially young foreign girls like our current drippy Tibetan au-pair Weh Ling.

And if she didn't work, where would we be? And, more importantly, where would Simon's lucky Euro 2012 Union Jack underpants be? Certainly not in the microwave where the idiot girl put them to dry! Honestly, don't they teach them anything in those Himalayan monasteries?

AND, one last thing, Cherie – it's not only the home mums who are called "Yummy". Some of us career girls have been described, quite often actually, by our male colleagues as "working yums"!!! Modesty forbids me from saying it was yours truly!!

● *Polly Filler's new book, "Yummy Money" (Johnson and Pearson, £19.99) is now on sale in all good supermarkets.*

BREATHTAKING ASCENT OF K2

by Our Mountaineering Staff **Ben Nevis**

A BRITISH citizen has won plaudits from around the world for his dizzying ascent of the K2 tax avoidance scheme.

K2, based in Jersey, has presented a huge challenge to those climbers who lacked the brass neck to opt out of actually paying any tax at all. Undaunted, and using nothing more than his nerves, the former comedian Jimmy Carr took time off from presenting satirical television programmes about greedy bankers on Channel 4 and climbed dizzying heights of humbug to achieve the target of 1 percent of income. He then immediately climbed down again as soon as it was pointed out on the front page of the Times.

Those tax avoidance schemes in full

K2 Investors are given a "loan" by offshore scheme allowing them to dodge tax.

K9 Investors put all money into robotic dog firm and recoup it 9000 years in the future when the Doctor shows up

KD Lang Investors give all their money to gay Canadian singer-songwriters

KFC Investors store funds at the bottom of an extra-large Bargain Variety Chicken Bucket, where HMRC will never look for it

KKK Roomy cloaks and headgear allow for comfortable storage of millions of pounds *(That's enough Ks. Ed)*

PM criticises hypocrisy

● David Cameron has criticised the comedian Jimmy Carr for his hypocritical stance on tax. "He's saying one thing and doing another", said the Prime Minister. "That's morally unacceptable and clearly a job for a politician.

"It would be like me saying Jimmy's tax avoidance is wrong but Gary Barlow's is right because he is a Tory supporter! Jimmy dontchajust hate him? Gary dontchajust love him. Byeeeeee!"

PAY: INLAND REVENUE
ONE PER CENT OF EARNINGS

BIRCH

TAKE THAT!

The Tax Avoiders

THE REVENUE says they cost the UK £4.5bn a year. The Chancellor says the most aggressive of them are morally repugnant. *The Times* reveals the secrets of the thousands of wealthy people in Britain who pay as little as 1 percent income tax using aggressive accountancy methods – part of the tax avoidance industry that costs the country billions of pounds.

An investigation by *The Times* has discovered that a comedian called Rupert Murdoch who owns a company called News International has for years used every sort of tax loophole and off-shore tax avoidance scheme to deprive the Revenue of billions of pounds.

The TV funny-man, famous for catchphrases such as "I don't recall that, Lord Leveson," and for his slapstick routine with a cream pie ending up in his face, has used numerous *(You're sacked, cobber. Ed.)*

● *Prime Minister attacks Carr's "straightforward tax avoidance". He says, "It should be complex, like all my friends' schemes".*

O-K2!

ISSUE 1317 ● 12 JULY 2012 ● £1.50

WHERE THE HOTTEST CELEBRITY BANK ACCOUNTS ARE HOLIDAYING THIS YEAR...

GABBY LOGAN's perfectly formed money turns a few heads as it romps on the beach

HAS IT PUT ON WEIGHT? Relaxing beside the pool in the Cayman Islands, it looks like **GARY BARLOW's** cash has piled on the pounds again...

Why We Must Have An EU Referendum – But Not Yet

WRITES **EVERYONE**

ONE thing on which the whole country is agreed is that the British people must be allowed to pronounce on our future relationship with Europe in a referendum.

Nothing can be more important than to allow the British electorate to decide on the greatest political issue of our time.

Are we to stay in the EU? Are we to leave it? Are we to renegotiate the terms of our membership?

These are the burning questions which cry out for an immediate answer, and on which every single man, woman and child in Britain is fully entitled to cast a vote.

BUT NOT YET.

Right across the political spectrum, from David Cameron to Ed Miliband, from the Daily Telegraph to the Guardian, from Will Hutton to Will.i.am, from Eddie Izzard to Eddie the Eagle, from Cheryl Cole to Old King Cole, the entire nation is at one.

Morning, noon and night, they think of nothing else but the vital need to stage a referendum on Europe as soon as possible.

BUT NOT YET.

As Prime Minister David Cameron yesterday told cheering MPs, "As you know, I am 100 percent behind the need for Britain to have a referendum on Europe.

"Indeed, I believe this so strongly that I am proposing that we should have an immediate referendum to allow the British people to decide on whether or not we should have a referendum."

Mr Ed Miliband said that he was happy to support the idea that there should be a referendum on having a referendum.

But he was at the same time quick to caution the prime minister that it would be inadvisable to hold such a referendum "until the time is right".

Speaking for the UK Independence Party, Mr Nigel Farage said, "I fundamentally disagree with having a referendum immediately. We should have had one 40 years ago, before I was born."

Scientology is not about brainwashing

Whatever you say, Tom

Ladies Semi- Quarter-Finals

(Round Three)
Donchalova v. Arenchasickova

THIS match had Centre Court literally on their seats, as the partisan Wimbledon crowd took Donchalova to their hearts, whilst booing Arenchasickova for her loud grunting and repetitive ball bouncing.

The first set was all Arenchasickova's, as she powered her way through with her unsportingly unreturnable serves and overly muscular baseline shots.

However, the match turned in the second set, as the crowd got behind the petite, pretty blonde Donchalova whose graceful deep shots and deft eating of a banana won the hearts of an appreciative middle-aged male journalist. *(You're fired. Ed.)*

Arenchasickova won 6-0, 6-1, and will go forward to play the winner of the match between the unseeded Neverurdova and the Chinese wild card entry, Hu Shee.

The Eye's Controversial New Columnist

The columnist who grabs hold of the cat's tail, and doesn't let go

This week I am very angry at this praise for so-called Andy Murray. Speaking as a baby *(see photo)*, I can inform Britain that he will always be the runner-up. I can't believe the country is deluding itself into thinking he's a world-class crybaby! Yes, I grant you, Mr Murray started blubbing incredibly strongly, with a good flowing style and brilliant nose-running all over the place but, as always with British sportsmen, the head goes down, the plucky grimace comes out and the tears are completely wiped out in a matter of minutes! I'm afraid he will always be a runner-up to myself, the true British champion, who can produce world-class bawls for hours on end, on grass or on lino, and am now in fierce training for the Olympics; my parents are cheering me on by crying as (*cont. p. 94*)

BBC REVEALS NEW HEAD

By Our BBC Staff **Bill 'Fearne' Cotton**

New head

THE new head of the BBC was unveiled today and amazed observers by being very similar to the previous head.

"It's a bald head belonging to a white middle-aged man," said one outraged licence-payer (Peter O'Bore).

There had been speculation that the head might have had long hair and worn lipstick but, as it happened, the BBC Trust chose the conservative option of what they called "a safe pair of glasses".

Supporters of the new head said that it was in fact completely different from the previous head.

"Look! There's no beard and no stubble which means the head has a clean-shaven chin on which to take abuse from the Daily Mail."

Outlining his plans for his new headship, the newly head-hunted head said:

"I plan to be attacked by everybody before I've even started."

GOD PARTICLE FOUND

by Our Science Staff **Nils Boring**

IN WHAT is being hailed as the most astonishing breakthrough in scientific history since Leonardo da Vinci invented the parachute, scientists at CERN today announced that they were "99.99997 percent certain" that they had at last discovered the long elusive "God particle".

Using a giant £100 billion super-telescope inside the Large Hadron Collider, experts were delighted to discover unmistakable evidence for the existence of a mysterious entity which, as one said, "Explains the Big Bang, the cosmos and anything else you can think of."

The telescope identified the electronic image, reproduced below:

LATE NEWS

Scientists all over the world were quick to hail the discovery of the so-called "God" particle as "little short of a miracle". "This discovery," they said, "opens up the opportunity for so many new lines of research that none should ever be short of a grant again."

Another scientist confirmed that, "We can now envisage a whole new parallel universe of funding which will keep us all extremely comfortable for the foreseeable future."

OSBORNE – UPBEAT ON ECONOMY

I can clearly see the recovery

EU-phemisms

"The whole of Europe is speaking German now"

LATEST AUSTERITY RULES

Wir sind kaputt

"Our economic policy shows how we can work together and defy petty national stereotypes"

The Greeks have been irresponsible, the French capricious, the Germans autocratic ... er ... er ...

"We will not allow a single country to leave the eurozone"

ECB

There'll be at least three

"The economies of the eurozone are becoming increasingly competitive"

My bailout is bigger than your bailout

"We have two distinct plans of action for the eurozone"

LATEST EURO CRISIS SUMMIT

Germany coughs up or we all go bust

EXCLUSIVE TO ALL PAPERS

DIAMONDGATE Day 94

Everyone To Blame, Says Everyone

by Our Financial Staff **Robert Pestonaircontinually**

IN a dramatic twist to what they are already calling "the greatest financial scandal since the South Sea Bubble", everyone was last night pinning the blame for whatever it is that is supposed to have happened on everyone except themselves.

Mr Bob Diamond, the former CEO of Barclays Bank, said, "It wasn't our fault. We were told to do it by the Bank of England".

Said the Bank of England, "It wasn't our fault. It was the Government who told us to do it."

A spokesman for the last government, Mr Ed Balls, said, "It wasn't our fault. It was those bankers who put us up to it. They even suggested that we change our name to New Libor, which we did."

BANKING CRISIS

I keep trying to withdraw £20 million and it won't let me

BOB DIAMOND 'SHOCKED'

by Our Banking Correspondent **Liz Bonus**

BOB Diamond has admitted that he was shocked to discover the extent of banking practices taking place in some of his most profitable criminal divisions.

"I would describe the people carrying out this banking as a few good apples who were certainly not representative of the vast majority of Barclays investment bankers," Bob Diamond told MPs.

"These idiots were driven solely by a love of savings and investments, and they should be ashamed of themselves."

Bob Diamond also expressed his sadness at being forced to resign from Barclays, saying the money had meant everything to him.

"People say it must have been the job, but it was never about the job, it was about the money. Loads and loads and shed-loads more of lovely money.

"Being separated from the money that I have loved and dedicated my life to will be the hardest part of all this."

OH NO! IT'S A SUMMERY EXECUTION!

THOSE BORS IN FULL

LIBOR	London Interbank Offered Rate
EUROBOR	Nigel Farage
COLOSSALBOR	Will Hutton
LIBORIS	London International Bonk Rate
NEW LIBOR	Party full of liars and bores
TREBOR	Sweet manufacturer known for making a mint (see Libor)
TWELVEBOR	Shotgun of the type senior bankers won't be using to do the decent thing

Han-z-z-zard

Parliamentary debate on the implications of the alleged fixing of the Libor rate

Rt. Hon George Pot, Chancellor of The Exchequer *(Yew-on-the-Turn, Con)*: It's all Kettle's fault! He's a big fat crook!

Rt Hon Kettle, Shadow Chancellor *(Brown's Bottom South, New Libor)*: No I'm not! YOU are the crook, Pot!

Pot: You're the bankers' bum chum, Kettle!

Kettle: You're the Barclays' bitch, Pot!

Pot: How dare you?! Apologise at once, Kettle!

Kettle: How dare YOU! YOU apologise at once, Pot!

Pot: Won't!

Kettle: Shan't!

Pot: I'm telling Mr Deputy Speaker on you!

Kettle: Not if I tell him on you first!

Mr Deputy Speaker: This is a disgrace. The public expects better of their elected representatives. Can we try and improve the level of debate?

Pot: It's all Kettle's fault!

Kettle: I blame Pot!

House erupts in delighted shouts of "Boo!", "Hiss!", "Shame!", "Resign?", "When's lunch?", as MPs on both sides forget what the debate is about and let bankers off the hook entirely.

ALL-PURPOSE

The Home Hadron Collider

Amazing scientific miniaturisation breakthrough allows you to discover the secrets of the universe in the privacy of your own home. Now you too can find the elusive Higgs Boson Particle!

- Self assembly
- Fits average size living room

Price €2billion

● **AUSTERITY SPECIAL** ●

REALI-TV

The UK's cheapest reality television show – featuring you in your own living room!

Simply stick the reflective film on your plasma widescreen TV and you can watch yourself watching yourself watching yourself! Or get the neighbours round and make a party of it! Hours of real life TV fun with **no** cost!!

● *Says TV's Nancy Dell'Olio, "With Reali-TV I can watch myself all the time! I am so sexy even Sir Trevor Nunn thinks so!!"*

99p

SPEED LOVERS!

SCALEXTRIC
'The Chris Huhne Set'

All the fun of traditional wheel-to-wheel miniature motor-racing, but with a Lib Dem twist!

Race around breaking the speed limit in the Energy Secretary's vehicle whilst being pursued by police in panda car!

SET INCLUDES: ● 2 cars ● 1 speed camera ● 1 miniature wife to take blame

Price: £1,000 (or six points)

Ladies! Put your worries *behind* you with

Pippa Pants™

Yes – now you too can draw admiring looks from all the men in the room – just like Pippa Middleton! These dynamic, dual-panel action control pants made from 100% polysamsonite are guaranteed to turn any woman into a derriere darling!?

Price: £2,759 per pair

Size: Small, medium, large, American

Plays "I was glad" by Sir Hubert Parry ♪

JUBILEE

INTRODUCING THE

My-Husband-and-iPhone™

Recreate the enduring splendour and majesty of 60 years of monarchy with this limited edition mobile phone fit for a Queen.

With its bejewelled, diamond-studded case and gold-style finish, the My-Husband-and-iPhone™ will transport you to a world of palaces and regal ceremony as you tell your partner you're on the train or play 'Fruit Ninja'.

Choice of bell ring tones: Westminster Abbey, St Paul's Cathedral, St George's Windsor

£299.99 per month

JUBILEE BALCONY

Get into the Diamond Jubilee spirit with this ornate facsimile scale model of Buckingham Palace balcony. Lovingly crafted by 9-year-old Chinese labourers, you'll feel like a Queen as you wave regally to loyal subjects on the street.

Jubilee balcony not load bearing. Using Jubilee Balcony could result in severe injury or death

£399.99 plus P&P

👑 ### JUBILEE POOP-*E͞R* SCOOP-*E͞R* 👑

FOR 60 YEARS the Queen has been cleaning up the mess, and not just from the Corgis! Now you too can be just like Her Majesty – when Fido does his business, you sort it out royally!

Plays: *Sir Edgar Elgar's 'Poop and Circumstance' March No 1.*

£39.99
(Does not include poop)

YES, IT'S THE FLOATILLA™

Enjoy all the Pomp and Circumstance of the Royal Diamond Jubilee Thames Pageant from the comfort of your own bath! This totally authentic miniature FLOATILLA™ includes 1:94 scale replica Royal Barge in breathtaking detail with life-like figures of HM the Queen, the Duke of Edinburgh and the Duchess of Wessex.

PRICE £979.99 (Bath water not included)

OLYMPIC

ACTION MAN – OLYMPIC SECURITY GUARD

It's the dead of night and the call comes through – Action Man has to be re-deployed from Helmand to check handbags at the Olympic Stadium in Stratford!

HOURS OF FUN with the most highly trained and deadly car park assistant in the world! String-activated voice says: *Can I see your ticket, please, Madam?*

£2012

Protect your air space with your own

Rooftop Surface-To-Air Missile System™

Easy to install, no planning permission needed, this state-of-the-art, Iranian built, Smart Multiple Rocket Launcher attaches easily to your TV aerial or satellite dish, allowing you to shoot down any of the following:
● Rogue Olympic defence missiles
● Dangerous debris from shot-down passenger aircraft
● Annoying pigeons.

£2,012,000 (spare missiles not inc)

FIZZY DRINK FANS!

Don't let the killjoy sponsorship police ruin your Olympic day with the

FAKE COKE CAN COVER

This ingenious aluminium device looks like a genuine can of Coca Cola™, but is actually a holder for **YOUR** fizzy drink of choice!

*Fits **ALL** drinks, including: Pepsi/Irn Bru/Lucozade/ 7 Up/Lager/Cider/Meths.*

Price: 20p for 12

DIY Do-ers!

Authentic Usain Bolts

These unique bolts may look like ordinary household screw-based accessories.

BUT they are the only bolts in the world to have been approved by the fastest human being on the planet.

Be the envy of your friends as you display a couple of Usain Bolts™ on your workbench!!!

Made from forged Polysamsonite alloys.

Price: £201.2 (per Bolt)

DIARY

NANCY DELL'OLIO: THE MEN IN MY LIFE

WILLIAM GLADSTONE: It was a long, long time ago. I was so very, very young. He was the Prime Minister, but I barely recognised him. We met at a party. I was so much more famous than he would ever be, and I think that's why he rushed over to meet me. He looked distinguished but nothing special, just another bald guy in a suit and high collars.

It was during his fourth Premiership. I asked him what he was up to, and he replied he was hard at work on the Second Home Rule Bill.

It was then that I felt those ice-blue eyes lock on to me. It was a look of shock mixed with desire – I could tell in an instant that he was already obsessed with me.

The white-hot laser of his stare met my eyes and seemed to strip me naked as he argued for a legislative assembly in Dublin with 103 members combined with a council with just under fifty councillors.

I was electrified. Willie may have been 84 years of age at the time, but to me, he was a teenager.

It was a very passionate relationship. I taught him all he knew about politics, and Willie taught me the secrets of the human heart. He was mad for me, but in the end, I had to tell him I had had enough of wrestling with those high collars of his, and so sadly we went our separate ways.

ALBERT STEPTOE: As a Virgo, I have always been attracted to older men, and Albert was definitely someone very, very special.

I was very, very young. We met at an international antiques fair. I turned to see this brilliant, important man looking back at me. I knew, as only a beautiful, formidably intelligent woman can, that in that split-second he was transfixed with desire. His eyes met mine. My eyes met his. Our eyes introduced themselves, and went out on a passionate date together.

Albert told me he owned an international store filled with the most divine soft furnishings, fine antiques and expensive *objets d'art*. He told me he was also the owner of a race-horse. He promised that if I joined him, we would ride everywhere together in his horse-drawn carriage, waving to all my fans as we passed by.

Sadly, after Albert took me to his home, I suddenly realised that our love – the most perfect love the world had ever known – was destined not to last. I am interested only in a man's soul, not in his worldly possessions, but, as a Virgo, I realise there must be limits. There was a tear in my eye, or very nearly, as I told Albert that I could no follow him along the road he wanted to travel. You see, I preferred Bond Street.

VICTOR MELDREW: I always made Victor so very happy. It was my natural intelligence that made his face light up. "I don't BELIEVE it!" he would say, as I told him at length and in fabulous detail my plans to make our world a better place through my exclusive contacts with international statesmen, sporting heroes, top grade celebrities and captains of industry.

Victor instantly recognised me as a woman like no other. I taught him to fly like a bird, soaring higher and higher with his Nancy. Yes, I taught Victor the meaning of *Amore*.

He had never met such a warm-hearted woman before, a woman so full of common sense. How do I know this? Because every time I opened my mouth and issued my pearls of wisdom, Victor would sigh in amazement and say, "In the name of SANITY!"

METHUSELAH: They say Methuselah was 969 years of age when he finally left us. But if that was so, he was a very young 969. In fact, my presence in his life gave him a new youth, a new inner meaning, a new zest, so that, at the time of his death, Methuselah could easily have passed for a man in his early 950s.

Before we met I had barely heard of him, but was vaguely aware that he was quite well known and had even got a mention in The Bible. I had been told, too, that he knew God Almighty, though to be honest not as well as I. To be frank, Methuselah was only on a nodding acquaintance with God Almighty, whereas I was an intimate, whispering hot suggestions into His ear before He had to make one of His dreary old pronouncements.

How well I remember the time my eyes locked with Methuselah's, across a crowded room! Earlier that day, after a period of intensive meditation, I had got in touch with my inner child, so I had arrived at the party wearing tiny shorts and a teenage vest that gave my gorgeous bust plenty of room to breathe and be happy.

When I leaned my body across Methuselah – he looked so marvellous in his wheelchair – the effect was electric. He immediately clutched his hand to his chest and his breath emerged in more and more rapid gasps. At that moment, I knew there was nothing for it but to straddle my young and passionate body over his and to give him The Kiss of Life. By doing so, I gifted him five more precious minutes on this gorgeous planet of ours. No words passed between us – they didn't need to! By moving his arms frantically to and fro, Methuselah was able to communicate his feelings in the language of love before he sadly breathed his last.

As told to CRAIG BROWN

Olympic Torch Relay

Day 994 – The Flame Reaches America

By Our 4,000-strong Olympic Relay Staff

Sally Sooper (for it is she): And welcome back to the 994th historic day of the iconic journey of the sacred flame from ancient Greece to London, via 8,000 cities, towns and villages in 24 different countries. Two days ago the flame was held high by Sir Engelbert Humperdinck on the top of Ben Fogle in Scotland. Yesterday it was taken by an Air Sea Rescue team to the tiny islet of Rockall. And today it's been brought back by hot-air balloon in the shape of a Coca-Cola bottle to the headquarters of the main sponsors of the torch relay, McDonald's, here in New Neasden, Arkansas, in the USA.

And we're going live to our reporter on the spot, Jilly Gosh, who is interviewing the next carrier of the historic flame, Mr Ronald McDonald IV, the chairman and CEO of the iconic beefburger company.

Jilly Gosh (standing outside huge golden arch with small man dressed as clown): Mr McDonald, you must be terribly proud to have been invited to carry the torch on behalf of Britain and the people of the United Kingdom?

Mr McDonald (for it is he): I feel part of history. I am overcome with the honour and privilege of my historic role in bringing the sacred flame all the way from ancient Rome to England-land…

When we got the contract to be one of the major sponsors, I had to insist that I should be allowed to select one of the runners in this iconic, historic and incredible journey on behalf of mankind… I could think of no one more appropriate for this great privilege than myself. That's why I am now going to use the Olympic flame to light this giant barbecue on which we are about to cook 10 million of our historic and iconic Big Mac burgers…

(Cont. Day 9,994)

"Are you authorised by the Olympic Committee to use their logo?"

TORCH AT WINDSOR

Get that thing out of here – we've already had one fire

TONY BLAIR GUEST EDITS PRIVATE EYE

WE are proud to announce that after his successful guest editorship of the Evening Standard, Tony Blair has become the first prime minister in history to be invited to edit Private Eye, Britain's foremost satirical fortnightly evening magazine.

Mr Blair welcomed our suggestion and immediately set about producing a list of ground-breaking articles and news stories.

Eye staff wait for Mr Blair's photo opportunity to end before they go off to do some proper work

He also recruited an awesome list of glittering contributors from amongst his friends, including Sir Bob Geldof, President George W. Bush, Rupert Murdoch and the late Colonel Gaddafi *(surely Nigella Lawson?)*.

Mr Blair himself writes a trenchant editorial, arguing persuasively that Britain needs a new leader, with the charisma, experience, gravitas and all-year tan necessary to rescue the country from its present vacuum

Senior Eye journalist Glenda Sands shows Tony Blair what a computer screen looks like

of effective political direction.

As Mr Blair puts it, "No one can doubt that since 2007 Britain has completely lost its way. Our economy has been allowed to disintegrate, our voice in Europe has been marginalised and we no longer count for everything on the world stage.

"None of this would have happened," Mr Blair emphasises, "if the country had remained true to itself under the benign guidance of a leader with charisma, gravitas, experience and an all-year tan."

Mr Blair has also commissioned a series of articles from the legendary political analyst Alastair Campbell, covering many of the major political issues of the day, such as:

■ *"How Tony Blair brought peace to Northern Ireland"*

■ *"How Tony Blair brought peace to the Middle East (particularly Iraq)"*

■ *"How Tony Blair brought Africa out of poverty"*

■ *"How Tony Blair brought the Olympic Games to London"*

and

■ *"How Tony Blair would be happy to accept a £100 million-a-year job solving all the world's problems".*

Mr Blair took part in all editorial conferences, even down to choosing headlines, photo captions and the magazine's famous front cover, showing a picture of himself

Mr Blair jokingly suggests to the proprietor's son, Evgeny Gnomedev, that, since his father is the 94th richest man in Russia, he might be interested in employing a distinguished and respected former British prime minister on some mission of international importance for an honorarium of, say, £10 million a year

with the satirical bubble, *"I'm the real heir to Blair".*

These exhilarating days in the Eye offices have brought home to us that Mr Blair could well have been one of the most brilliant journalists of all time, had he not been the greatest Prime Minister and world statesman of the 21st Century (or arguably any other).

(Reproduced from the "How To Spoon It" supplement of the Financial Times)

SIR PETER OSBORNE
Bart.

As George Osborne's father, you must be aware of the enormous public interest in your spoon collection...

Indeed I am and it's a great pleasure to talk to you about it.

Do you have a favourite spoon?

I'm rather fond of this long-handled silver spoon which belonged to Queen Victoria. I use it to eat my caviar in the evening, which I have delivered from Fortnum's.

Have you always been a lover of the spoon?

I find it very hard to resist the lure of a beautifully crafted spoon. At the moment I've got my eye on the most wonderful designer spoon made by the Italian master-cutler Francesco De La Spooni.

How much is that going to cost?

Well, it's about £19,000, but then you have to treat yourself once in a while, don't you?

Do you think your son would be embarrassed by such extravagance at a time when he is appealing to us all to tighten our belts?

Not at all. George is a broad-minded sort of chap and, besides, he stands to inherit my spoons, so he can't afford to be too critical. Ha ha ha.

Has anything amusing ever happened to you in connection with a spoon?

Ha ha ha. I know what you press people are like. You're not going to catch me out like that. Ha ha ha.

NEXT WEEK: *Charles Glass, "Me and My Glass"*

LORDS REFORM LATEST

Hands up. Who wants to be elected?

"Mere material wealth pales in comparison to your generous gift of dance"

The Alternative Rocky Horror Service Book

No. 94 A service to celebrate the delaying of a decision by the Synod as to whether or not it is the right time to consecrate women as Bishops of the Anglican Communion.

The President (Archbishop Rowan Pelling, *for it is he*): Brothers and sisters, we are gathered together today for the 89th time in the last year to come to a firm resolve that we are not going to make a decision on the consecration of our sisters to the episcopate.

All: Let us give thanks that we have managed to duck this issue yet again.

(Or they may say)

All: Come off it, Beardie, stop running away from this one – it's time you bit the bullet.

Reading

*From the Letter of
St John to the Laodiceans*

And so it shall be written that those who do serve and love the Lord best are those who are neither hot nor cold on any great matter, but very sensibly remain lukewarm, coming down neither on one side nor the other, but agreeing to avoid trouble by postponing their decision until some future time, which may be the ending of the world or eternity, whichsoever may come soonest.

Reader: This is the word of the Lord Archbishop.

All: Indeedy-doody.

The Breaking of the Promise

The President: We now come to the solemn moment when we recall that we were going to get round all the objections which have been made to a female episcopacy, by devising a formula whereby parishioners could insist on a male "flying bishop".

All: We do so remember.

The President: Well, now several brothers and sisters from the more traditional wing of our Communion have raised a further objection even to this very sensible proposal, by arguing that a "flying" bishop cannot be so qualified if he himself was consecrated by a female (and therefore "non-flying") bishop who had thus broken the Apostolic Succession which, by definition, must exclude female bishops, whether "flying" or not. And furthermore...

All: Z-z-z-z.

Hymn

There shall then be sung Hymn No. 94 (from Hymns Modern and Modern)

"The day thou gavest, Lord, is ended
And fortunately we still haven't come to any Decision on this one."

The Dismissal

The President: Go in Peace, and see you all again next month. Amen.

All: And A-women, but only at some future date.

© Society for the Promotion of Christian Discord.

"Don't just laze around the house – get off your arse and look for benefits"

From The Message Boards

Members of the online community respond to the major issues of the day...

Falkland Islanders request special passports

I see the plucky Falkland Islanders are in talks with the government about having their own special passports with "Falkland Islands" on the cover, to express their pride. Good luck to them, I say. What about you guys? – **Bogbrush**

I fly the flag of Saint George from my flagpole, with sticky tape in the shape of a cross. (The white flag symbolises our surrender to the "red tape" of the EU.) I have never been abroad, but I have ordered a passport in order to show my solidarity with our kith and kin in the South Atlantic. I shall be removing the words 'EUROPEAN UNION' and replacing them with 'FALKLAND ISLANDS AND GIBRALTER'. Let the Busy-Bottoms of Brussels try and stop me. – **Metric_Martyr**

so so glad the forklander's r standin up 4 there right's and the pengin's that live in the iland ☺ many pengin's r gay these day's its been shown in the zoo's that it is natural and consent-ing ☺ it wuld be a disaster if the argie's come back and make the pengin's life a misery ☻ – **Darling_Deneyze**

I have a fantastic idea. Put a penguin picture on all the passports. Then the England team could have a penguin on their shirts and when they play Argentina in the European Cup in the summer it will shame them into treating the Atlantic penguins with respect. – **Lassie_Louise**

I see that Sean Penn is sounding off again about British colonialism in the Falklands. I wonder what this posturing prima donna would say if the gay penguins were left to the tender mercies of the Argentine army? – **Last_taxpayer_standing_in_the_LiebCon_socialist_paradise**

not bein funy but y do they call him a premadonna when madonna divorced him year's ago? – **Hayley_321**

Time to end the disastrous demographic experiment. – **Sword_of_Truth**

S O there's a new survey proving that women have now got higher IQs than men! Tell me something I don't know!

Those of us on the frontline of the multi-tasking modern maternity matrix, balancing the tightrope of caring and career, know that us wummies (working mummies) need an IQ of over 170 merely to survive!

And if you don't believe the stats, just look at the menfolk in the Filler household! How many brain cells does it take to sit slumped on the sofa watching *Kim Kardashian's 100 Best Thongs* on Sky UK Atlantic Living Dave Plus 4 presented by Keith Lemon?! I'm talking about you, useless Simon, since, being a bloke, you are probably too dim to work it out for yourself, just like you can't work out how to use the Dyson – it's a vacuum, Simon, rather like your head!

Ok, I'm being unfair (but not to my pea-brained partner!). There **are** some exceptions to the "low male IQ" rule.

My toddler Charlie's latest school report from St Upid's Free School For

POLLY FILLER

Differently Gifted Children (Chair of Governors, Toby Jugg) said that Charlie was so intellectually challenging to the teachers that they thought he should be taught at home and not come into school ever again! Pretty bright **boy**, eh?!

But, sadly, the truth is that the majority of the male species have been hopelessly left behind by the advance of women who **are** smart cookies and don't just **bake** them! (Btw, I tweeted this bon mot last week and it instantly trended amongst the Twitterati, being retweeted more times than anything by Justin Bieber, Caitlin Moran, Barak Obama or even Stephen Fry!)

A ND you know what proves conclusively that women like yours truly have got "High-Qs"? (Excuse me a second while I tweet that one!) We're smart enough to employ other women – in my case, the miserable girl Wee Ping from Xin Jiang – to do all the drudgery. Meanwhile, **we** go out with our girlfriends and get completely "clevered" on a bottle or two of Veuve Cl-IQ-ot (sorry, must twit!).

● *Follow Polly @pollytwitter*

OLYMPIC ALERT!

Just put down the Pepsi can and no one will get hurt

G4S CALLED IN AFTER ARMY CUTS

by Our Outsourcing Staff **Phil Ranks**

THE Government has admitted that the shortfall in troop numbers caused by defence cuts means that it will have to outsource many of the Army's traditional tasks to the private security firm G4S.

Said Defence Secretary Phil Hammond, "The fact that we are sacking a fifth of the Army to save money does not pose any problem because we can spend the money we've saved on hiring the services of a top-quality private firm to carry out such day-to-day tasks as Trooping the Colour, fighting in Helmand and providing security cover for major international events such as the Olympic Games."

When asked by MPs how he could justify his new policy in light of the admission by G4S that they

hadn't managed to recruit anyone to do the work, Mr Hammond said, "This is not a problem. If G4S cannot recruit enough private soldiers to replace the missing G4S security men whom we had hoped would provide security cover to the Olympics, then we will simply call in the police, if we can find enough of them now that we have outsourced most of their duties to G4S."

Those Racial Insults Explained

Choc-ice	Black person who is white inside
Tim Westwood	White person who is black inside
Dale Winton	Orange person who is pink inside
Nick Clegg	Yellow person who is blue inside
David Cameron	Blue person who is yellow inside
Boris Johnson	Blue person who would be happy to be inside female person of any colour (*That's enough, Ed.*)

Han-z-z-zard

Select Committee for Media, Publicity and Self-Promotion

Keith Vaz (*Hinduja West, Lab*)**:** We have the huge pleasure today of welcoming to our Committee Mr Nick Buckles, the chief executive of G4S, so that we can demonstrate just how clever we are and, incidentally, guarantee extensive coverage of ourselves on tonight's TV news.

All: Hear, hear!

Enter bespectacled man in suit with silly haircut, looking rather worried.

Vaz: I will ask my honoured colleague, David Winnick, to begin the humiliation of our witness.

David Winnick (*Bordering-on-Insufferable, Lab*)**:** Mr Buckles, would you describe your company's performance as the most shambolic, inept, outrageous, shocking, useless example of incompetence ever seen in the history of the world?

Mr Buckles: That's probably a fair description of it. I'm very sorry.

Winnick: Answer yes or no, Mr Buckles.

Vaz: The witness will answer the question. Are you a totally incompetent idiot or not?

All: Answer, answer!

Buckles: Yes, if you say so.

Ms Lorraine Fullbrook (*Total, Con*)**:** That's simply not good enough. Are you guilty or not guilty? That's what the entire nation wants to know.

Buckles: Guilty.

Vaz: How dare you come here and admit that you've got it all wrong – thus deliberately depriving this Committee of the chance to set new Olympic records for self-righteousness.

Buckles: I can only apologise for my previous apology.

Vaz: Well, now we've forced that humiliating admission out of you, Mr Buckles, I think we've done enough to get star billing on Mr Jon Snow's admirable Channel 4 News at the very least. So, sadly, there won't be any time for our Committee to interview any further witnesses in an effort to find out which of our fellow politicians were responsible for awarding this ludicrous contract to your firm in the first place, and why they only noticed yesterday that your firm had been cocking the whole thing up for the last five years.

"Do you accept that summer is a humiliating shambles?"

HSBC DRUG SHAME

by Our Banking Staff **Charlie Snorter**

THE world of drugs was rocked to its foundations today by the revelation that some top international drug cartels have been closely involved in seedy business dealings with high street banks.

Said one leading Colombian drug baron, "This could ruin my reputation. This drugs business has been in my family for generations..." He sniffed, "And to know that our money has been laundered by such unsavoury characters brings shame upon us all."

He sniffed again, "I would like to apologise to all our valued customers on the street – but, hopefully, their minds have already been so scrambled by all the other banking scandals that they won't have a clue what's going on..."

Said one top HSBC banker, "It's like, wow, hey, this is some crazy shit. Woo!" He continued, "Don't mess with us – we're extremely unpleasant and we could ruin you. Remember, we know where you live – because we mis-sold you a mortgage."

THAT BORIS JOHNSON OLYMPIC ODE IN FULL

Cripes and blimey, what ho chaps,
Let's wish the Games success,
And barring one or two mishaps,
It won't be a total mess.

We've got running and jumping and hockey and tennis,
And fellows who are good with an oar,
We've got fruity girls like Jessica Ennis,
And the volleyball lovelies — Phwoar!!!

So welcome to you, Johnny, Frog, Jap and Hun,
And let the Games begin!
And when the vital race is run,
May the best man (Bozza) win!

Translated from the original Greek by the late Sir Harold Pindar.

'I SALUTE TOP BRITISH CYCLIST,' says Bradley Wiggins

ONCE in a generation comes a man who rewrites the history books, a gentleman who rides a bike and whose name begins with B.

The total dedication and the passionate commitment to winning is what sets an Olympian like Boris apart. He is arguably the finest British politician in the history of the world.

That is why I and the rest of Britain say "Allez Bojo!", as this glorious figure cycles on his victory tour of London, wearing his iconic yellow hair, inspiring an entire generation to get on their bikes and vote Conservative.

© B. Wiggins 2012

"I'm afraid the north-south divide runs right through the middle of the house"

The Medici Mail

ONE FLORIN

Friday, July 27, 1490

Put it away, Madonna, we've seen it all before!

BY OUR ART STAFF BRUNOSEWELLI

There was outrage yesterday when the Madonna publicly bared her breast in a painting by Leonardo da Vinci.

The crowd were shocked at this explicit display and one onlooker said, "At her age she really should be covering herself up rather than exposing herself in public.

"It's not as though she's like a virgin any more. Oh, no, apparently she still is."

On Other Pages
● *Rolling Stones – Farewell Tour of Tuscany 2*
● *Shard of Pisa Opens – office space still to let 3*
● *Unfunny cartoon by Raphael 97*

WORLD'S OLDEST MUSICIANS BANNED ON HEALTH AND SAFETY GROUNDS

by Our Concert Staff **Gertrude Jekyll** and **Edward Hyde-Park**

THOUSANDS of fans breathed a sigh of relief last night when two of the world's oldest musicians had their life-support systems switched off after going on for longer than anyone could be expected to tolerate.

Sir Big Macca, 107, had been summoned to the stage by his fellow performer, the 94-year old **Bruce Nospringchicken**, to sing the legendary 1923 hit *Twist, Shouts and Leaves.*

But after they had been singing for two and a half hours, Health and Safety officials insisted that both men should be rushed to hospital to spare the audience any further suffering.

A spokesman for the concert organisers said, "It is utterly outrageous for these little Hitlers to prevent two great legends going on all night just because we had agreed to end the concert at a particular time."

He continued, "Don't these jobsworths realise that musical history was being made? Never before have Big Macca and Nospringchicken ever been heard on the same stage, and it is only a tragedy that they never did so while either of them could still sing."

CHILCOT REPORT 'MAY NOT EXIST'
Shock Government Revelation

BY THE LATE **W.M. DEEDES**

THE much-discussed report into the Iraq War, which threatened to destroy the government "within 45 minutes", has yet to be found and a report last night claimed there was no physical evidence that it had ever existed.

Said one security analyst who wished to remain anonymous (the late Dr Kelly), "Once again, our intelligence has let us down. We thought it was only a matter of time before the Chilcot Report was deployed with devastating results, but at present there is no sign of it."

He continued, "Its existence may have been exaggerated and sexed-up by government spin doctors hoping to make the case for war on the hated Middle-East tyrant, Tony Blair, and his toxic henchman and diarist, Chemical Ali Campbell."

Exclusive to all newspapers
An Apology
The Olympics

IN THE last few months, in common with all other media, we may have given the impression that the London 2012 Olympics was in some way going to be a complete disaster with the capital city becoming a nightmare due to hopelessly inadequate transport systems and the requirements of national security turning London into a police state, albeit one very badly managed by hopeless and overpaid private security firms. We further may have led readers to believe that all the Olympic tickets had gone to commercial sponsors or overpaid Euro bureaucrats and none to genuine fans who were in any case totally uninterested in the overblown and overhyped Olympic games and the artificial and irrelevant construct called "Team GB". Headlines such as "On Your Marks, Get Set, Go Abroad!", "Take A Running Jump, Lord Coe," and "Yes Britain Wins Gold In The Bore-a-thon," may have unwittingly reinforced the idea that we were not 100% behind the efforts of LOCOG and the IOC.

We now realise, in the light of the past week's events, that there was not a jot or scintilla of truth in the above. We are now happy to accept that London 2012 is the most important single event in British history since the Battle of Hastings in 1066.

We would like to make clear for the record that Britain is no longer broken and is, on the contrary, a warm, relaxed, happy and successful nation at ease with itself which has rediscovered its self-confidence and spirit in a festival of optimism, pride and goodwill for which there is only one word – "Absolutely Bloody Fantastic."

We hope that today's 94-page Olympic Special Wrap-Round and 994-page Olympic Gold Supplement, will compensate for any misunderstanding to which our previous coverage may have given rise. The headline on today's paper should, we trust, serve as a mere balanced and rational response to the London 2012 phenomenon.

GOOOOOOOLD!!!!!

We apologise for any confusion caused to our readers or indeed ourselves. © *All newspapers*

NEW ROLE FOR ARMED FORCES

by Our Defence Staff **Max Capacity**

IN THE modern world, fighting men and women have to be ready to adapt to a changing strategic environment and the latest defence review has highlighted some of the areas in which troop deployment has to be rationalised to meet the demands of the 21st Century.

From now on, Britain's soldiers, sailors and airmen will be expected to:
- fill up empty seats at Women's Taekwondo quarter finals
- search themselves before filling up empty seats
- fill up empty shops in Oxford Street
- fill up empty restaurants in Covent Garden
- fill up commuter trains at London Bridge
- fill up empty seats at the Wednesday matinee of The Mousetrap
- fill up empty seats in late night House of Commons debate on reform of the House of Lords
- fill up House of Lords to vote down reforms voted in by themselves (see above)
- fill up empty seats at Edinburgh Fringe student productions
- fill up empty seats at Job Centre
(That's enough, Ed)

STOP PRESS
Falklands Invaded whilst Troops at "Warhorse".

Nursery Times

Friday, August 10, 2012

FAIRY GODMOTHERS THREATEN TO STRIKE FOR REMAINDER OF OLYMPICS

by Our Magic Staff **Tinkerbel Mooney**

THERE were angry scenes outside the Olympic village yesterday, as Fairy Godmothers picketed the stadium and threatened to down wands for the rest of the games.

"Talk about tube drivers, it's us that need a raise," said one delightful old lady in a tiara, "we've been granting wishes left right and centre for the whole games and we need overtime."

"Too right," agreed another lovely silver-haired lady in a taffeta ball-gown. "How many more wishes does Britain want us to grant? We've done gold medals for everyone, Andy Murray winning at Wimbledon, we even did Boris Johnson being strung up by his testicles.

"We're working far too long hours and we want someone to look after us for a change.

"I mean, what next? You'll be wanting us to get Louise Mensch to leave the country next."

"It's the Paralytics"

Another British Record Smashed

by Our Olympic Staff **Sandy Pitt**

Britain's amazing record-breaking streak continued last night as GB achieved the longest double dip recession in the country's history.

George Osborne, who took the Gold (and the Silver and the Bronze) told reporters, "It's incredible. Even in my wildest dreams, I never saw it turning out this badly. It just shows what you can do with 100 percent determination and 0 percent talent."

He continued, wiping away the tears, "I'd like to thank everyone who has contributed to this

extraordinary low point in my career – to Dave, my coach, who has been with me every step of the way, even though he denies it now."

The double-dip is a very difficult discipline requiring a unique combination of stamina, inflexibility, and all-round uselessness. Team GB is indeed fortunate to have such an extraordinary performer as Ozzy "Austerity" Osborne to represent it.

Experts believe he now has every chance of pressing on to even greater depths in 2016 and beyond.

BORIS WELL-HUNG

"It's not my first embarrassing mishap with a zip, eh ladies?"

ST CAKES' HEADMASTER PRAISES 'PUBLIC SCHOOL MEDALLISTS'

by Our Education Staff **Tanya Gold**

THE headmaster of the Midlands independent mixed fee-paying school (and registered charity) St Cakes (motto: "Quis Paget Entrat") today defended the proportion of old-boy medallists from his school.

"We are of course very proud of our Old Cakeian Olympians," he said. "We were delighted with Johnny Abercrombie-Fitch's silver in the Men's Equestrian Water Polo, which was a fine effort, particularly after what his horse Mr Mishap did in the pool!

"As for Charlie Huntley-Palmer-Tomkinson and Sandy Sebag-Monte-Python – well, their gold in the Coxless Coxed Coxing Sculls was little short of breathtaking, particularly as their best event at school was the classical Trireme.

"And lastly, can I mention Julian Manolo-Blahnik (now Juliette Manolo-Blahnik) who played such a blinder in the Transgender Beach Volleyball and I think may have caught the Mayor of London's eye!"

Mr Kipling concluded, "I know there has been some outrage over the fact that 50 percent of Britain's gold medallists went to one school, ie St Cakes. Well, I share this outrage. It should be closer to 90 percent!"

St Cakes' fees are now £27,000 per term.

PARANORMAL OLYMPICS

Cluff

EMPTY, DESERTED... THE OLYMPIC EFFECT

By Our Man in the Pub Watching Television and Pretending He is Really There **Lunchtime O' Lympics**

Huge areas of the nation's newspapers were completely empty of content as the Olympic Games got into its full swing.

Said one reader, "It is incredible. There's not a real story in sight. I went from page one to page 94 and saw no one, apart from fruity girls getting in and out of boats and swimming pools."

"Where *has* all the news gone?" asked another, "Is it all on holiday? There aren't even any silly season stories to be seen."

There was speculation in the

industry that this "news desert" would have a major impact on sales.

"We think they are going to go up."

ON OTHER PAGES ● Wrap Around Cover of Fruity Cyclist *p.1* ● Free Giant Poster of Fruity Beach Volley Ball Girls *p.2* ● Special Supplement Addressing Problems of ECB's Response to Worsening Spanish Debt Crisis *(shurely shome mishtake? Ed.)*

Notes&queries

What is the derivation of the 'Peloton'?

● Mrs Cavendish is of course quite wrong to suggest the word Peloton comes from the French "poulet de tonne" – literally "a heavy chicken". Her assertion that the rules of cycling make it necessary for there to be a "basket of riders" constituting the so-called "heavy chicken" is understandable, though, as it happens, entirely inaccurate.

Peloton derives from the Prussian general, Wilhelm von Peloton, who at the famous Battle of Hoy in 1869, amassed a large body of troops a mile behind his front line ("Das Peloton") believing that he could launch a perfectly-timed attack as the enemy grew tired. Unfortunately, the battle was lost long before the Peloton finally turned up. *The Rev J.R. Pendleton, Drome, Somerset.*

What is a Keirin?

● I have watched from the sidelines for quite long enough as the ill-informed debate has raged in your columns. May I put the record straight?

Your correspondent Professor Froome, from Frome, comes closest in his claim that the word is of Japanese origin, but is wrong to suggest it comes from "Kirin", meaning giraffe, even though stretching out one's neck could indeed enhance a cyclist's chance of winning.

But no, the truth is much more prosaic. The word comes from an incident in the Tokyo Olympics of 1964. A Scottish competitor called Kieran McKnightly arrived for the cycling race on his motorbike. His hosts, thinking he had misunderstood the rules of the competition but not wishing him to lose face, insisted he compete on his motorbike, which became known ever afterwards as the Kieran or, as the Japanese misspelt it, the "Kierin". (McKnightly actually finished a disappointing 5th in the final due to running out of petrol on the last bend.) *E.R. Wiggo, Burnside.*

Answers to the following please:

What is repechage?
What is Dirty Wind?
Why are medal winners given flowers?
What is the correct height for a Huffington Post?

OPENING CEREMONY DAZZLES

By Our Fireworks Staff **Danny Boyling-Point**

THERE WAS widespread agreement that the opening ceremony of the destruction of the Syrian City of Allepo by the Assad regime was a dazzling success.

"Seeing the helicopter gun-ships raining down shells on heavily populated civilian areas was an evocative way to tell the story of Western impotence against powerful oil rich countries," said The Washington Post.

"I didn't understand everything that was going on, because it was so foreign-looking, but minor quibbles like that aside, this was a triumph," said the Vancouver Chronicle.

"It was bonkers but brilliant, at times you couldn't believe savagery on this scale existed, but Assad pulled it off. Bravo!"

said the Sydney Morning Herald.

"The amazing cauldron of fire shooting up into the sky in the heart of the city had me whooping for joy!" tweeted Kim Kardashian.

The bits about the international community doing nothing about it were carefully edited out by the NBC coverage, as they were not tailored to the US audience.

Fleet Street's Gold Meddler??!!

■ THE Olympics – donchajus-luvem?!! I tell you, Mister, this hardened hackette has been forced to shed a li'l tear or two whenever our beefy boys and gorgeous gals start a-weepin' and a-wailin' as they listen to Gawd Save Her Maj on the podium!? All together now, boo hoo hoo!!?!

■ THE Olympics – donchajus-luvem!?! I tell you, Mister, when I see our smilin' soldier boys checking our

bags or those cheery volunteers in pink tellin' us all where the nearest toilets are, this hardened hackette has had to shed a li'l tear or two!!? All together now, boo hoo hoo!?!!

■ THE Olympics – donchajus-luvem?!! And donchaluv Clare Balding, Jessica Ennis, Bradley Wiggins, Danny Boyle, Mo Farah… (**You're fired**, Ed.)

Byeee!!

"That's quite some food intolerance, sir!"

DAILY TELEGRAPH   Friday, 10 August 2012

Letters to the Editor

The Olympic opening ceremony

Sir, – Am I alone in finding the Opening Ceremony of the Olympic Games a totally disgraceful travesty of the history of our once great country? Only the most rabid Marxist, such as Mr Danny Boy, could have dreamed up such a twisted, communist caricature of the events of the past 200 years. It was all very well to have begun with milkmaids and sheep dancing round the maypole and playing cricket with morris dancers as they sang Jerusalem, but we were then treated to the spectacle of this rural idyll being destroyed by a gang of evil top-hatted capitalists led by Sir Kenneth Branagh, polluting the countryside with their vile factory chimneys, to such an extent that the nation's children became violently ill and had to be cured by the National Health Service led by Mary Poppins. We then saw all this good work being threatened in turn by a towering dark figure who was clearly intended to be Margaret Thatcher, who was in turn destroyed by thousands of loutish and unkempt popular singers, such as Sir Paul McCartney, and who were supposed to have ushered in a new golden age of freedom, happiness, equality, liberty, fraternity and all that rubbish. Worst of all was the deliberate act of treason committed against Her Majesty the Queen, by forcing her to jump out of an aeroplane at the age of 86 – no doubt in the hope that she would fall to her death, allowing the Olympic organisers to declare Britain as a socialist republic, headed by its new People's President Mr Boris Johnson.

Everyone responsible for this disgraceful farrago should, in my opinion, be arrested by members of the Armed Forces, whose contribution to our victory in two World Wars (not to mention our liberation of the Falklands) was so noticeably and shamefully ignored in five hours of the most turgid agitprop I have ever been forced to sit through since the death of the late Joseph Stalin. I remain, Sir, yours utterly disgusted,
Sir Herbert Gussett,
Dunwatchin, Great Adlington, Poole, Dorset.

The Guardian   Friday August 10 2012

Letters and emails

The Olympic opening ceremony

I was utterly sickened by the feeble, feel-good propaganda of the so-called "opening ceremony" of the Olympic Games, with its uncritical support for the British establishment in all its forms. From the singing of right-wing Christian anthems such as Jerusalem and Abide with Me, to the delight the organisers clearly took in showing heroic and downtrodden workers being beaten up by smiling top-hatted capitalist bosses, every box was ticked. Totally predictably the Queen representing an effete and totally outmoded monarchy was allowed to rehabilitate herself via attachment to celebrity culture in the shape of James Bond, who instead of being exposed as a torturer and mass-murderer for the state intelligence apparatus was portrayed as a fawning lackey of a totally decadent feudal system... er... and most disgraceful of all was the attempt to glorify the NHS without a single reference to the fact that it is collapsing thanks to Tory cuts.

And when the right-wing organisers of this sickening travesty of the real people's history of Britain, led by Mr Frankie Boyle, had the nerve to show us a towering figure representing Margaret Thatcher as the hero of the story, I thought I was going to be in need of a visit to one of those hospital wards which, thanks to her, have all been closed down. As to the billions of pounds wasted on those fireworks, every penny of that could have been better spent on building desperately needed badger sanctuaries and windfarms, which were so disgracefully omitted from the reactionary pastoralist fantasy picture of Britain's countryside given at the beginning of the whole perverted (cont. p. 94).
Dave Spart
The Toynbee Estate, Hutton Way, Crouch End.

⭕⭕⭕ Private Eye's Complete ⭕⭕⭕ Up-to-the-minute 24/7 Results Guide to the Latest Olympic Results

Man Wins Event

A man has just won an event. The other men did not win the event. The man was very happy. The other men were not so happy.

Woman Wins Event

A woman has just won an event. The other women did not win an the event. The woman was very happy. The other women were not so happy.

Men and/or Women Win Event

Some men and/or some women have just won an event. They were very happy. The other teams were not so happy.

⭕⭕⭕ Exclusive Private Eye ⭕⭕⭕ First Olympic Interviews In Full

Eye: How do you feel?

Athlete: Fantastic/Amazing/Unbelievable

Eye: What was the atmosphere like?

Athlete: Unbelievable/Fantastic/Amazing

Eye: What was the crowd like?

Athlete: Amazing/Unbelievable/Fantastic

Eye: Would you like to cry now?

Athlete: Yes.

Those top ten films of all time as voted by the nation's most irritating film critics

1. Black and white film
2. Black and white foreign film
3. Colour foreign film
4. Foreign film that no one has seen
5. Unfunny silent comedy film
6. Film noir
7. Film noir et blanc
8. Japanese film with German subtitles
9. Turkish film that doesn't make sense even with subtitles
10. They Flew to Bruges (*shome mishtake surely?*)

BRAVE BECKY GOES DOWN FIGHTING

by Our Crime Staff John Invernick

In a disappointing performance last night, British heroine Rebekah Brooks attempted to defend her title (News of the World) and herself against charges brought by the Crown Prosecution Service.

Despite going to any lengths, plumbing the depths, and threatening to sink or swim, brave Becky failed to convince the judges that *(careful, Ed.)*

She thanked her team for all their hard work, although she insisted she had no idea what they were doing.

Becky is best known for the Murdoch Crawl where she (*cont. p. 94.*)

OLYMPIC COMMITTEE DISCUSSES EMPTY SEATS FIASCO

POLICE LOG

Neasden Police Station

8.00hrs All officers were redeployed from normal duties onto Operation Twitterwatch, monitoring suspicious and criminal tweeting activity over the Olympic period. 115 60-inch plasma-screen television sets were installed in the station, to enable officers to correlate tweets and Olympic-related events.

10.30hrs First major tweet alert recorded while officers were watching heats of the 20-kilometre kayak time trial at Hampton Court. PC Brondesbury picked up tweet from member of the public, Kev94, sending message concerning failure of GB's competitor Matt Coracle to qualify for quarter-finals because of collision with marker pole. Our "Tweet Detectives", headed by Sergeant Hainault, subjected the message to forensic examination and concluded that its wording "stick pole up your arse Matt you wanker and then drop dead" was a clear incitement to murder and an offence under the Terrorism and Allied Offences Act 2006.

11.45hrs Armed "Tweet Swat Team" was ordered to track down and arrest the suspect Kev94. Following exhaustive investigation (i.e. asking Twitter to give us his address), the suspect was identified as Kevin Snott residing at Flat 412, the Tessa Jowell Estate, Poundstretcher Road. 317 officers surrounded the suspect's address and after breaking down the door of his bedsitter, managed to disarm him of his mobile phone, which was retained as evidence, and placed him under arrest. Suspect put up a brief resistance, necessitating use of taser and pepper spray, but no live rounds were required, in accordance with the new guidelines on Avoidance of Killing Civilians Unless Strictly Necessary.

13.15hrs Suspect was detained in custody at Neasden Central and charged with five criminal offences relating to his tweet before being discharged.

13.30 – 21.00hrs Officers celebrated successful operation by continuing to monitor Olympic sporting events in alternative venue viz the Slug and Lettuce in Pricerite Avenue.

21.00hrs Duty Officer Sgt Kennington returned to station to find emergency answerphone full of messages from members of public reporting incidents of burglary, theft, assault, domestic violence, and murder. Sgt deleted all low-priority requests for assistance, i.e. all of the messages and tweeted to followers: "Police cannot cope with huge increase in workload due to Twitter Crime".

"He says that everybody of his generation will be infamous for 15 minutes"

GERMANY TO LEAVE THE EURO

by Our Economics Staff **Stephanie Flounders**

WORLD markets yesterday went into total meltdown when German Chancellor Angela Merkel announced in Berlin that Germany would be the first country forced to leave the eurozone.

"Frankly," she told a huge crowd gathered in front of the Reichstag, "we Germans can no longer tolerate this nonsensical system.

"Everyone assumes that it is Germany's duty to pay the debts of all the weaker economies in the eurozone, such as Greece, Portugal, Ireland, Spain, Italy, France and, let's be honest, all the others.

"But there is only so much money even in Germany, and we simply have not enough to continue pouring it into this bottomless pit.

"There are only two possible alternatives to this impossible situation. Either the other sixteen countries in the eurozone head for the exit, leaving Germany as the only member state remaining in. Or, Germany regretfully does the sensible thing and gets out, leaving all you useless, lazy, inefficient, spendthrift, greedy, sad, pathetic non-German people to rot in the cesspit that you have deliberately created for yourselves by indulging in an orgy of crazy and reckless spending of money you have not got whilst expecting the bill to be picked up by us hard-working, decent, honest, thrifty and above all German Germans."

As Mrs Merkel completed her speech to her adoring audience of 80 million people, the crowd broke spontaneously into a rousing chorus of "Deutschland Über Alles".

In later trading the Euro lost 99.99 percent of its value and is now worth one Zimbabwean dollar.

Can Coalition Survive?

We are in total agreement...

...that we disagree about everything

Lines on the Success of the London 2012 Olympic Games

By William Rees-McGonagall

'Twas in the year of Our Lord Two Thousand and Twelve
That Alex Salmond feared his dreams of glory he'd have to shelve,
With Team GB succeeding as never before
In bonding the nations of the UK, numbering four:

Athletes from England, Scotland, Wales and Northern Ireland
Were cheered in their efforts by everyone in the entire land
Unalloyed indeed was the British public's joy
At the triumph of Scottish heroes like cyclist Sir Chris Hoy
And this applied most keenly to tennis-playing Andy Murray
To adopt whom the spectators had previously not been in a hurry

Yet their wild applause when he won the gold
At centre court against Federer was a wonder to behold
And when bold Murray wrapped himself in the Union Jack
It seemed that for the country there could be no going back.

In fact, the only loser in the entire jamboree
Seemed to be the portly leader of the SNP
For wily Alex Salmond the self-appointed heir of Wallace and Bruce,
Had hoped the Olympics could be put to his own personal use,
But his high hopes for causing national division were blighted,
As the Kingdom showed itself to be disappointingly united.

Because from the tip of Land's End to distant John O'Groats
One cry went up from the people's throats
From furthest Ballymena to distant Abergavenny
There was truly very little dissent, if any,
And all the guid folk sang the most popular national anthem by far,
Mr McCartney's classic Na Na Na Na Na Na Na.
(Surely "God Save The Queen"? Ed.)

© W. Rees-McGonagall

POLLYANNA (formerly Polly Filler)

WELL, wasn't that the most ab-so-bloody-lutely fan-bloody-tastic two weeks of all time?

I tell you, it's the best thing that has happened to this country in its entire history and I don't mind telling you that it has changed all of us for good, forever and for the better. It is as though we all suddenly woke up to find ourselves nicer, happier and finer human beings, casting off the old habits of corrosive cynicism and discovering a joyous positive approach to life.

I watched endless sport on television with my wonderful partner Simon on the BBC's 94 red button channels and we laughed, cried and sang together. My toddler Charlie was so inspired by our Olympians that he has taken up BMX Underwater Dressage at a local club and after a couple of sessions is already a more disciplined, more content and more appreciative child.

And as for me, why, I have taken up the challenge and have decided to volunteer!

Yes – I have volunteered our new Chinese au pair, Fi Shi, to work unpaid at weekends to look after Charlie so that *I* can go to the gym and concentrate on emulating the real star of the Olympics, the modern female role model and feminist icon, Jessica Ennis.

I want a stomach like hers, girls, and nothing is going to stop me. Isn't it all too wonderful?

© Pollyanna, *The Voltaire Press*, 2012.

PUTIN 'CLEMENCY' FOR PUSSY RIOT

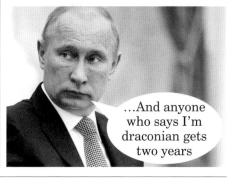

...And anyone who says I'm draconian gets two years

RAIL OPERATORS HIT 100% PUNCTUALITY TARGET

by Our Train Staff **Mervyn 'Off' Peake**

PROUD rail franchise chiefs today proudly defended their record in terms of punctuality.

Said one, "We have stuck to our timetable and the huge fare increases have arrived bang on time." "Every year it is the same", said another, "our customers can't believe that we can deliver this level of consistency. But we have.

"One hundred percent of the massive price hikes that we promised have made it safely to the passengers' wallet exactly at the time we scheduled – ie, just when they are feeling hard up with inflation rising and winter on its way."

Said one regular commuter, "This latest rise is an outrage. I would fall off my seat if I only had managed to get one."

"How much?! I want to buy a ticket not the flippin' franchise!"

A Post-Olympic Message to the People of Britain from The Mayor of London

Yes, it's the Bojobot

WHAT ho, fellow Olympians. Wasn't London 2012 the best thing that's ever happened in the history of this country, if not the world?

That's one of Bojo's rhetorical questions because we all know what the answer is. And I don't want to blow my own trumpet, but there can't be any doubt as to who won the gold medal among our country's Political Team GB.

Yes, I know my old friend the prime minister turned up for one or two events looking a bit like that plucky fellow from the Marshall Islands who took three days to finish the 100 metres. And I know we Brits love a loser, Dave, but there are limits!

No offence, but I'm not sure it wouldn't have been wiser to stay at home in Number Ten watching the Women's Beach Volleyball through a pair of binoculars from your upstairs window, which is certainly what I would have done if I'd been in Number Ten which, for some reason, I am not yet.

Anyway, the Olympics were a huge triumph for all of us who played a part in that unforgettable drama – the athletes, the organisers, the volunteers, the spectators, the torchbearers, the singers, the dancers, Sir Danny Boyle and, of course, the inspirational and charismatic Mayor of the host city.

But, as we all know, the important thing now is the legacy.

How do we carry forward the spirit, the daring, the organisational genius, the optimism and the sense that anything is possible in the new can-do Britain that is only waiting to be awakened by the right kind of visionary leadership?

Well, here's my own humble offering to get the ball rolling – Bozza's 10-point plan to ensure that the Olympic legacy lives on forever:

1. The building of a huge new island in the Thames, Boris Island, as the perfect site for the world's largest airport, Johnson International.

2. The construction of a network of elevated cycleways throughout London to enable millions of commuters to use their "Boris bike" to pedal from one station to another in a totally safe and environmentally-friendly way.

3. The introduction into all London schools of four hours a week of compulsory "Boris Dancing" (as seen in the unforgettable closing ceremony of the Olympic Games). This way a new generation of young Londoners will grow up fitter, healthier and more culturally attuned than any previous cohort of Britain's youngsters.

4. The building of thousands of charging points for my planned new fleet of Boris Minor electric cars, which will transform London into the cleanest, greenest city on the planet.

5. The transforming of Britain's political landscape in the same way that east London was regenerated by replacing all that was old, run-down and useless with all that is new, exciting and Olympic. In other words, "au revoir" (as we Francophone Olympians say) to Dave, and "bienvenue" to "le Grand Fromage des Olympiques Vingt-Douze", moi-même!

6-10. Bojo will think of these other points when he's Prime Minister!

© *"Beano" Boris (now incorporating the Dandy)*

Daily Mailograph

Friday 24 August 2012

Let's have more of the volunteer spirit

IF THERE is one thing we have learned in the last few weeks it has been that the great British tradition of offering your services without thought of financial reward is alive and well.

Can we not be inspired to carry this forward into all areas of our national life?

There is no doubt that British industry benefits hugely from the selfless efforts of unpaid interns who do so much to keep the cost-base low enough to stimulate growth, generate profit, facilitate dividends and keep executive pay and bonuses at an acceptably high level.

But why stop with interns?

Surely nearly all jobs could be done on a voluntary basis, particularly in the public sector, which would give British business a huge boost – with labour costs disappearing and pay disputes a thing of the past, reinvigorated firms could once again produce the sort of wealth creation last seen in the cotton boom of *(cont. p. 94)*

LEGACY SHOCK

What's it feel like winning twice?

You'll never know

"Yes, here we believe in competitive sports"

UPFRONTERS
SPECIAL
Olympians on the piss

We may be third in the medal table but we are first **under** the table! Yes, welcome to our tribute to our generation-inspiring boys and girls who are drinking for Britain! We present Team G'n'T! and hope their spirit provides a real tonic to the whole nation!

Champagne a-**Hoy** for **Sir Chris** (centre) – he knows how to handle *bars*! And has heptathlete Jessica (left) had one over the eight? Is she asking Scotch-loving **Andy** (centre): "Anyone for **Ennis**?" *(This is terrible, Ed.)* And is our golden middle-distance runner (not in the picture) enjoying one **Mo Farah** the road? Or another double!? *(No, he's a devout Muslim, Ed.)*

That's **Charlotte** of booze for horsy Miss **Dujardin** (centre left). Maybe she could *recycle* some of it with Miss **Pendleton** (bottom right) who is certainly **Victoria**-us in the drinking sprint!? *(This is really appalling, Ed.)* And can I spot our women rowers (centre right) out of their sculls? Are **Katherine** and **Anna** in **Grainger** of consuming too much **Watkins** Red Barrel? Or maybe it's our triathlon hero brothers **Alastair** and **Johnny** (centre-bottom left and right) knocking back the Newcastle **Brownlee**?? No? Perhaps it's our party **Princess** and one of our men behaving **Bradley**?! Time **Zara** gave him a **Wiggin** over the amount of vodka he's drinking! He's wheelin' around and the room and she's *(No, this is too bad. You're fired. Ed.)*

How Government Has Developed

PAST	NEAR PAST	PRESENT

Leadership	Management	Compliance

LORDS REFORM New Plan Shock

BY LORD COE OF SEB

IN A dramatic new proposal for revising the Upper Chamber, Lord Coe has put forward a radical plan in which all the Team GB athletes who won a medal in the recent Olympics will be honoured by being elevated to the peerage.

The resulting 65 new peers will have a number of distinct advantages over the 750 current incumbents (who will retire immediately) claimed Lord Coe, as he outlined the benefits in his Red, White and Blue paper:

● Many of the athletes are very good at sitting down.

● Lord Farah of Mobot will be very good at running things very fast.

● Lady Ennis is an expert mult-tasker capable of doing seven things at once very well.

● Lord Wiggins of Sideburn is not a man for back-pedalling.

● Unlike the current peers, their incredible popularity means that anything that they do will be applauded by "People GB".

● They are clean of performance-enhancing drugs, such as Chateau Lafite 68, Glenlivet 62 and Viagra 94.

● Er...

● That's it.

Those most popular children's names in 2012

The Office of National Statistics, having nothing better to do, has published its eagerly-awaited list of the most popular names given to children in the last week.

Boys		Girls	
1.	Mo	1.	Jessica
2.	Usain	2.	Laura
3.	Wiggo	3.	Zara
4.	Sir Chris	4.	Victoria
5.	Seb	5.	Somalia
6.	Harry	6.	Clare
7.	Boris	7.	Balding
8.	Daley	8.	Sporty
9.	Bradley	9.	Beth
10.	Mo (again)	10.	Queen Elizabeth II

© *Office of National Statistics.*

Fruity Boys Celebrate Results

by Our Exam Staff **Zilli Zeason**

THERE was jubilation amongst the nation's teenage boys as for the first time ever male A-level students outshone their female counterparts.

More fruity boys appeared in the newspapers than fruity girls, reversing the trend of the last thirty years.

Said one fruity boy leaping in the air and bearing his midriff as though he were a fruity girl, "I am delighted – I have got the place I wanted: the front page of the paper".

Not everyone, however, was pleased with the results. Said one middle-aged man, "There is clearly something wrong here. I do not expect to buy my newspaper on results day and be confronted with pictures of boys."

He continued, "If the fruity girls have not done well enough to appear leaping in the air on the front page, can we not have pictures of them weeping and consoling each other instead… but obviously still looking fruity?"

ON OTHER PAGES

● Pictures of Boys doing Usain "Lightning Bolt"
● Pictures of Boys doing Mobot
● Pictures of Asian 6-year-old boy with record 94 A* at A-level

YES, IT'S PRESIDENT ROMNEY!

Wife's astonishing tribute rocks Obama

by Our Tea Party Staff **Lunchtime No'Booze**

THEY are hailing it as the most astonishing political speech of modern times – a game-changer that could transform the political landscape for the next millennium.

In one brilliant flash of oratory, Mitt Romney's wife (*fill in name*) yesterday transformed her husband from a dull, colourless cypher into a towering and charismatic political giant who now looks odds-on favourite to enter the White House next November.

As 50,000 cheering Republicans roared their approval, Mrs Romney told them, "Mitt is a good man. He works hard and, I promise you, when he is elected he will really do his best to be a good President.

"That is why, in my opinion, the people of America should think very seriously about voting for my husband."

As Mrs Romney's message was beamed around the world, the Obama camp sadly accepted that the Presidential race was as good as over.

Said one White House staffer, "We had no idea that the Republicans had this secret weapon up their sleeve.

"When the President watched it on TV in the Oval Office I can tell you that he had his head in his hands and was weeping uncontrollably, with laughter."

ASSANGE TAUNTS HAGUE OVER EMBASSY BLUNDER

He threatened to force an entry without consent…

You're the expert, Julian

"Prithee, mercy – not the unpaid intern!"

ASSANGE FEARS BEING HELD IN SWEDISH DETENTION CENTRE

by Our Swedish Correspondent **Not Bjorn Yesterday**

FRIENDS of Julian Assange say the WikiLeaks founder fears being detained in one of Sweden's notorious IKEA detention centres.

"These brutal and desensitising IKEA facilities make Guantanamo Bay look like the Ritz," said one WikiLeaks supporter. "Once inside the labyrinth-like building you are deprived of natural light and forced to drudge round seemingly in circles for up to eighteen hours a day looking for a set of drawers, a kitchen unit and a side table while having an argument with your partner."

Swedish authorities insisted that by handing himself over to a self-assembly tribunal within an IKEA facility Julian Assange could be freed quicker, as the cases they build are extremely flimsy and fall apart within minutes.

CARRY ON BORIS

I've got your ball in my hand

Oo-er missus!

(Cont. from previous ad break for pizza)

Commentator *(possibly Jon Snow or Krishnan Guru-Murthy or Clare Balding or someone in a wheelchair)*: ...and now, as the umbrellas of progress

unfurl to face the hailstorm of ignorance, the giant apple of Newtonian physics explodes into a nuclear core symbolised by the man on stilts riding a bicycle with Galileo's lightbulb on his head, who represents

the Hadron Collider of destiny, colliding there quite literally with the Bill of Rights, on top of which is a man in a wheelchair who isn't Stephen Hawking, while a woman with blue hair in another

wheelchair waits patiently, suspended in mid-air, defying the gravity of the apple as eaten by Sir Ian McKellen, who quotes from the Tempest, bringing back memories from

Britain's golden past, such as the time Sir Kenneth Branagh quoted from the Tempest all those days ago wearing the stovepipe hat of industrial engineering and chewing on the cigar of wonder... And now, to symbolise that Channel Four is not discriminating against the Paralympic Opening Ceremony by treating it any differently from its normal programming, there will be a break for more irritating adverts.

(Cut to tacky commercial for GoCompare or those bloody meerkats)

THE EYE'S MOST READ STORIES

Nick Clegg's message to Paralympians

DURING a visit to the Olympic Village Nick Clegg has told Paralympic athletes he does not want their pity.

"As I walk around the village I meet a lot of athletes who say I must be so brave to do what I do," Clegg told the Paralympians, "but I say to them that overcoming the very real handicap of being Nick Clegg has always been what's driven me on.

"I don't think of myself as being 'special', and if you look at the opinion polls you'll see the people of Britain don't either."

'Olympic Parade' Announced

As G4S revealed it had lost £50m due to the Olympics fiasco, details were hurriedly announced of plans

"Aye, Jim lad, I can outrun any Captain in the Royal Navy"

to parade senior G4S executives through the streets of London.

"This will be a chance for the public to show their appreciation," said a LOCOG representative.

"Millions of joyous Londoners armed with rotten fruit and vegetables are expected to line the route as the executives travel in a wooden cart from Mansion House and along the Strand.

"In the grand finale, they will arrive in Trafalgar Square where they will suffer the ultimate indignity of a live concert featuring Jessie J, the Spice Girls and Sir Paul McCartney."

CLEGG IN LAST-DITCH APPEAL TO LIB DEM GRASS ROOTS

Look at the sandals, guys

'SILLY SEASON' STORY ON LOOSE IN ESSEX

By Our Rubbish Correspondent **Cat Litter**

REPORTS of a bank holiday silly story on the loose caused widespread panic throughout Essex.

"We think the traditional bank holiday story might have escaped from a nearby media circus," said one Essex caravan park resident, barring up his doors and windows.

"All we know is that there is a massive media pack roaming the country and we're scared to go out for fear of being asked if we're living in fear."

Responding to reports of a "screeching noise", Essex police were quickly scrambled, firing six

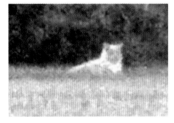

tranquiliser darts into Kay Burley as she rampaged through St Osyth High Street.

"Any threat posed by Kay Burley to local people is now at an end," said Essex Chief Constable Knacker, just before being eaten by a lion.

Your Cut-out-and-keep Guide To Wildlife Prowling Essex Streets

Ravenous man-eater with enormous mane

Lion

CLEESE MARRIES FOR 4th TIME

It's a silly walk up the aisle

Say Cleese!

This is an ex-wife!

She's a jewellery designer. She has designs on jewellery!

And now for something completely similar

© Hello and Goodbye Magazine 2012

"Don't worry, you're not the only one trying to find affordable childcare"

Does this picture prove Neil Armstrong's death was faked?

by Our Lunar Correspondent
Phil Outerspace

JUST moments after the death of Neil Armstrong was announced, a photo was posted on Twitter which conspiracy theorists say proves his demise was faked.

"The photo clearly shows Neil Armstrong stepping onto the surface of the moon when he is supposed to be dead, how is that possible?" said @conspiracynut11.

"The shadows and the reflection in his helmet prove without doubt that his death was staged on a soundstage in Burbank," said @toomuchtimeonmyhands.

"NASA claims this photo was taken on 20th July 1969, but we know that to be a lie because everyone knows the original moon

landing was faked," added @38andstilllivingathome.

Conspiracy theorists say they believe that far from being dead, 82-year-old Neil Armstrong has faked his own death as a cover for what he is really doing, landing on the moon to try and convince the world that the faked moon landing was in fact, a faked fake, and was real all along.

"This is one small conspiracy theory for nerds, one giant crock of s*** for mankind," tweeted @mikegiggler.

SHOCK NEW HARRY PHOTO

Stop looking at my chopper

67

SAYS

Harry's shame

We are not ashamed to be the only paper in Britain which dares to publish this picture of a 27-year-old man with his trousers off.

Repeatedly yesterday, the Sun was ordered by Buckingham Palace not to print this historical image.

Nudes international

But the Sun believes that it is a matter of the highest national importance that this picture is made freely available for all its readers to see – in defiance of those whose only concern is to crush free speech.

For a long time, the Sun has been at the very forefront of the fight for freedom in this country.

That is why so many of our brave journalists have been arrested and imprisoned by the ruthless agents of the state.

Naked greed

The Establishment, headed by the Royal Family, may be determined to silence us by any means at their disposal.

But let the message go out loud and clear to those who would muzzle the media and gag the champions of liberty.

What is at stake here is nothing less than a principle of the highest importance – our right to publish blurred pictures of royals with their kit off, in order to sell more copies of the Sun.

Nursery Times

········· · Friday, September 7, Once-upon-a-time · ·········

NAKED EMPEROR PICTURE PUBLISHED

by Our Royal Correspondent **Wee Willie Winkie**

HANS Christian Andersen last night defended his decision to print a picture of the Emperor in the altogether, the altogether, the altogether, as naked as the day that he was born.

"It's in the public interest," said Mr Andersen. "Don't get me wrong, I like the Emperor, but the public has a right to know if he has been very silly in his choice of new clothes *(cont. p. 94)*

WORLD'S MOST FAMOUS COW DIES

by Our Orbituary Staff

TRIBUTES poured in this week for the Cow Who Jumped Over The Moon who died peacefully in her field, aged 82.

The cow was fêted as being the first bovine ruminant to jump over the moon. There have been many subsequent lunar expeditions, but none have been quite as livestock-related.

A little dog, who covered the moo mission, said, "This was history in the making. When she orbited the moon's surface, it put a lie to the silly romantic notion that it is made of rock, and proved once and for all that it is, in fact, 100% gorgonzola."

Said Mission Commander, the Cat With The Fiddle, "In spite of her celebrity, she remained a very private and humble cow. Her first words will go down in history: *'This is one small jump for a cow, one giant leap for cowkind'.*"

On other pages

Lion spotted by witch in wardrobe "just a big domestic cat" **3**

Three blind mice win paralympic gold **4**

"I suppose we should have got together sooner to discuss Britain's looming energy crisis"

95

D I A R Y

Holy shit. My mouth goes dry just looking at him. He's so freaking hot.

He grabs my left foot, bends my knee and brings my right hand up to his left shoulder.

I gasp.

Watching and assessing my every reaction, he takes my right arm and moves it towards my left knee whilst avidly placing my left hand on my right elbow.

He pauses, waiting for me to calm.

"Good girl. Now place your hands and forearms flat on your thighs. Good. Now part your toes."

He narrows his eyes, one on either side of his nose, and continues.

"Move your right elbow so that it's parallel with your left ear-lobe."

Wow! I realise with a start that he's not going to stop at my right elbow. No – even now, he is grasping my left ankle in his right hand and starting to move it to my right shin, whilst at the same time taking my right buttock in his left hand and seeing if he can make it reach my right elbow, which still has my left hand on it.

"Excellent, Miss Steele!" he murmurs, moving my right shin to my left thigh before spinning me round triumphantly with his right arm, "Now look in the mirror!"

Exhausted, I gaze into his $75,000 Bulgari mirror bought from Macy's exclusive department store in Manhattan, New York, and gasp.

"Can you see what it is yet?" whispers Mr Grey, avidly.

"Some sort of hat?" I ask, dreamily. "Or maybe a lily?"

"No, Miss Steele! Can't you see?" he begs with manly irritation. "You're a swan!"

"Why, of course, Mr Steele!" I sigh in wonderment. He has folded me into a swan shape. It is then that I notice the tears streaming down his face.

"I had a very tough introduction to life," he sobs. "I don't want to burden you with the details."

"Don't tell me if you don't want to," I insist.

"Oh, all right then," he sobs uncontrollably. "When I was a little boy, my mother took no interest in me. She preferred to spend her time folding napkins into fancy shapes. I never got over it. Now I can only gain intimacy with a young lady if she lets me fold her like a napkin. I take her in my hands and fold her, fold her, fold her, until she is a suitable ornament for even the most splendid dinner table!"

FIFTY SHADES OF GROT

With that, he begins wiping his mouth on me, over and over and over again, spinning me up and down and round and round, left to right and any-old-how, firm and slow, then faster, faster, faster – rub, rub, rub – until we both collapse exhausted onto the floor.

Holy cow. I have never known a napkin like it. We are both wiped out.

When I wake, Mr Grey is at the piano, completely lost in the melody he's playing. His expression is sad and forlorn, like the music. His playing is stunning. He is able to use both hands at once.

"That was a beautiful piece," I say. "Bach?"

"Chopin. Prelude opus twenty-eight, number four. In E minor, if you're interested," he murmurs. "Perhaps best known for his nocturnes, Frederic Chopin is considered one of the great masters of Romantic music..."

When I wake, Mr Grey is still at the piano.

"Born in the village of Zelazowa Wola, in the Duchy of Warsaw, the young Frederic was soon to become a renowned child prodigy..." he continues. It all spurts out of him like a waterfall.

He tweaks the stem of his champagne flute with his expert hand and looks at it through his narrowed eyes. "Bollinger Grande Annee Rose 1999, an excellent vintage," he sighs.

How long can he keep going like this? No man before has ever bored me so stiff, so solid, his every shaft of verbiage thudding into me like a truncheon. Beneath his boorishness, I yelp and writhe, begging for mercy as he rampages across me with his cock and bull.

Holy shit – skip! I tell myself. So I pull off my lace panties and, leaving him at his piano, skip naked into the kitchen, my body bursting with an insatiable craving – but for what?. It craves one thing and one thing only. Something warm, gurgling, moist.

Yes! A cup of tea!

Jeez. I need it! Badly.

The kettle is electric. I glide my forefinger over its bulbous protuberance.

I press it. Upwards, upwards.

It comes alive in my hands. It lights up and leaps into action, quivering, growling, simmering, then bubbling as – oh! oh! oh! YES! YES! – it comes to the boil.

As the kettle moans and howls, my naked body knows instinctively what to do. The pressure is uncontainable, it wants to detonate.

Together, the kettle and I rush headlong towards the kitchen cabinet.

My needy fingers caress the box marked "PG Tips". I dive in and cup a tea-bag oh so tenderly in my hand before inserting it, firmly but gently, into the empty vessel that lies – beseeching, yearning, avid – below.

I tighten the handle of the kettle in my palm and will not let it go. I squeeze and squeeze.

I lift it.

And it is powerless to resist.

I tilt it, slowly at first, then faster, faster, with ever more urgent tilts.

Deep within its body, something cries out for release.

Ecstatically, the kettle empties itself into the cup, pounding the defenceless tea-bag over and over again. It shudders violently against the hard, unforgiving surface of the porcelain. Within seconds, the bag is left drained and satiated, aromatic liquids spilling uncontrollably through its moist perforations.

One lump.

Two lumps.

They plunge in, and breathlessly dissolve.

Inside, something stirs.

My teaspoon.

I moan. He groans.

He groans. I moan.

He moans. I groan.

I groan. He moans.

"How much longer can we keep this going?" I groan, moaningly.

"Only another 587 pages and we're done," he moans, groaningly.

As told to
CRAIG BROWN